VOCABULARY
FROM
CLASSICAL ROOTS

C

Norma Fifer ▾ Nancy Flowers

EDUCATORS PUBLISHING SERVICE
Cambridge and Toronto

Acknowledgments

Illustrations in *Vocabulary from Classical Roots—C* have
  been taken from the following sources:

*Catchpenny Prints. 163 Popular Engravings from the
  Eighteenth Century.* New York: Dover Publications, Inc.,
  1970.
1800 Woodcuts by Thomas Bewick and His School. Blanche
  Cirker, ed. New York: Dover Publications, Inc., 1962.
*Food and Drink. A Pictorial Archive from Nineteenth-Century
  Sources.* Selected by Jim Harter. Third revised edition.
  New York: Dover Publications, Inc., 1983.
Huber, Richard. *Treasury of Fantastic and Mythological
  Creatures. 1,087 Renderings from Historic Sources.* New
  York: Dover Publications, Inc., 1981.
The Illustrator's Handbook. Compiled by Harold H. Hart.
  New York: Galahad Books, 1978.
Men. A Pictorial Archive from Nineteenth-Century Sources.
  Selected by Jim Harter. New York: Dover Publications,
  Inc., 1980.
*Victorian Spot Illustrations, Alphabets and Ornaments from
  Porret's Type Catalog.* Carol Belanger Grafton, ed. New
  York: Dover Publications, Inc., 1982.
Women. A Pictorial Archive from Nineteenth-Century Sources.
  Selected by Jim Harter. Second revised edition. New
  York: Dover Publications, Inc., 1982.

Cover photograph: PhotoDisc/Getty Images

Printed in Benton Harbor, MI, in May 2013
ISBN 978-0-8388-2256-2

14 PPG 15 14 13

Contents

Preface

Vocabulary from Classical Roots encourages you to look at words as members of families in the way astronomers see stars as parts of constellations. Here you will become acquainted with constellations of words descended from Greek and Latin, visible in families that cluster around such subjects as the human being, kinds of mental activity, and aspects of daily life.

You will notice that Latin and Greek forms appear as complete words, not as fragments. Some alliances in word families are easily recognizable, but others may seem strange without your seeing the complete sequence of forms. Some Latin nouns are consistent, like *femina,* "woman," and *manus,* "hand," but others shift according to the way they are used in Latin sentences: *cor, cordis,* "heart," and *rex, regis,* "king." The principal parts of the verb "to love" are similar in form: *amo, amare, amavi, amatum.* But this regularity disappears in the verb "to bear": *fero, ferre, tuli, latum.* If you didn't know that these forms belong to one verb, would you believe that the English words *conference* and *relationship* belong to the same family?

This book can do more than increase your recognition of words; perhaps it will encourage you to study Latin or Greek. More immediately, though, it can remind you that English is a metaphorical language. By returning to the origins of English words you will move closer to knowing how language began: in naming people, things, and concrete actions. So enjoy visualizing the life behind the words you use every day, descendants of Latin and Greek, seeming almost as numerous as stars.

Notes on Using *Vocabulary from Classical Roots*

1. **Latin (L.) and Greek (G.) forms.** Complete sets of these forms help to explain the spelling of their English derivatives. Practice pronouncing these words by following some simple rules.

   To pronounce Latin:
   > Every *a* sounds like *ah*, as in *swan*.
   > The letter *v* is pronounced like *w*.
   > The letter *e* at the end of a word, as in the verb *amare*, should sound like the *e* in *egg*.

   To pronounce Greek:
   > As in Latin, *a* sounds like *ah*.
   > The diphthong *ei* rhymes with *say*; for example, the verb *agein* rhymes with *rain*.
   > *Au*, as in *autos*, sounds like the *ow* in *owl*, and *os* rhymes with *gross*.

2. **Diacritical marks.** Following every defined word in *Vocabulary from Classical Roots* is the guide to pronunciation, as in (dī ə krĭt′ ĭ kəl). The letter that looks like an upside-down *e* (called a *schwa*) is pronounced like the *a* in *about*. You will find a key to the diacritical marks used in this book on the inside front cover.

3. **Derivation.** Information in brackets after the guide to pronunciation for a word gives further information about the source of that word. For example, after **diacritical** (dī ə krĭt′ ĭ kəl), which appears under *dia* <G. "apart," would appear [*krinein* <G. "to separate"]. Thus, the word *diacritical* is made up of two words that come from Greek and means "separating the parts" and, consequently, "distinguishing."

4. **Familiar Words and Challenge Words.** Listed next to groups of defined words may be one or two sets of words belonging to the same family. You probably already know the Familiar Words in the shaded boxes. Try to figure out the meanings of the Challenge Words, and if you are curious, look them up in a dictionary.

5. **Nota Bene.** *Nota bene* means "note well" and is usually abbreviated to *N.B.* In *Vocabulary from Classical Roots,* NOTA BENE calls your attention informally to other words related to the theme of the lesson.

6. **Exercises.** The exercises help you determine how well you have learned the words in each lesson while also serving as practice for examinations such as the SAT: synonyms and antonyms, analogies, and sentence completions. Further exercises illustrate words used in sentences, test recognition of roots, and offer writing practice.

PART ONE

Who Am I?

The Person

Directions

1. Determine how the Latin or Greek root is related in meaning and spelling to each defined—KEY—word that follows it.
2. Learn the pronunciation and definition(s) of each KEY word, and notice how the words are used in sentences.
3. Practice using the varied forms of KEY words.
4. Build your knowledge with all the information given: Latin mottoes, Familiar Words, Challenge Words, and Nota Bene references.
5. Complete the exercises.

LESSON 1

Humani nihil a me alienum puto.
Nothing human is alien to me.—TERENCE

Key Words		
anthropology	egoism	humane
autocrat	feminism	humanism
automaton	feminist	humanities
autonomy	gynecology	misanthrope
autopsy	homicide	virile

HUMANUS <L. "human being"

1. **humane** (hyōō mān´)
   adj. Having the worthy qualities of human beings, such as kindness or compassion.

Familiar Words
dehumanize
human
humanitarian
humanity
humanize
inhuman

Challenge Word
humanoid

The International Labor Organization helps to ensure **humane** conditions in the workplace.

humaneness, *n.*

Antonym: **inhumane**

2. **humanism**   (hyōō′mə nĭz əm)
n. A philosophy in which interests and values of human beings are of primary importance.

The development of **humanism** in the sixteenth century changed the focus of English education from theological speculation to human achievements.

humanist, *n.*; **humanistic**, *adj.*

3. **humanities**   (hyōō măn′ə tēz)
n. Branches of knowledge concerned with human beings and their culture: philosophy, literature, and the fine arts, as distinguished from the sciences.

Although most of her college courses were in the **humanities,** she did graduate work in electrical engineering.

Challenge Words
anthropoid
anthropomorphic
philanthropy

ANTHROPOS <G. "human being," "man"

4. **anthropology**   (ăn′ thrə pŏl′ ə jē)   [*logos* <G. "word," "speech," "thought"]
n. The scientific study of the origins, cultural development, and customs of human beings.

Fragments of a human skeleton found in an Iron Age cave led to important discoveries in **anthropology.**

anthropological, *adj.*; **anthropologist**, *n.*

5. **misanthrope** (mĭs′ən thrōp′)   [*misein* <G. "to hate"]
n. A person who hates all people.

In Charles Dickens's *Great Expectations* Miss Havisham becomes a bitter **misanthrope** after being jilted on her wedding day.

misanthropic, *adj.*; **misanthropy**, *n.*

HOMI-, HOMIN- <L. "human being"

6. **homicide**   (hŏm′ə sīd)   [*occidere* <L. "to kill"]
   n. The killing of one person by another; a person who kills another.

   In *Arsenic and Old Lace* two elderly sisters commit **homicide** by putting arsenic in elderberry wine.

   homicidal, *adj.*

   NOTA BENE: The Latin stems *homi-, homin-*, meaning "human being," and the Greek word *homos*, meaning "same," look alike but have different meanings. The Greek *homos* gives us *homocentric, homogeneous, homogenize, homonym, homonymous,* and more than fifteen other words applying chiefly to biology and language.

VIR <L. "man"

7. **virile** (vĭr′ ĭl)
   adj. Having certain characteristics traditionally associated with masculinity, especially physical strength, vitality, and assertiveness.

   The main characters of Ernest Hemingway's novels are often **virile** men who risk danger in war or sport.

   virility, *n.*

GYNE <G. "woman"

8. **gynecology**   (gī′ nə kŏl′ə jē)   [*logos* <G. "word," "speech," "thought"]
   n. The branch of medicine dealing with disorders and treatment of the reproductive system in women.

   Gynecology is a promising field for medical students who are especially interested in women's health.

   gynecological, *adj.*

FEMINA <L. "woman"

9. **feminism** (fĕm′ə nĭz′ əm)
   n. The belief that women should possess the same political and economic rights as men.

The union president's **feminism** led him to demand equal pay for women who perform the same jobs as men.

feministic, *adj.*

10. **feminist**   (fĕm′ ĭ nĭst)
    n. A supporter of women's claims to the same rights and treatment as men.

    Feminists argued that the Equal Rights Amendment should be added to the U.S. Constitution.

AUTOS <G. "self"

11. **autocrat** (ô′ tə krăt′)   [*kratia* <G. "power"]
    n. 1. A ruler who has absolute or unlimited power; a despot.

    Elizabeth II cannot become an **autocrat** like her ancestor Elizabeth I because today the monarch's power is limited by Parliament.

    2. Any arrogant, dominating person.

    As company director she became an **autocrat,** making all decisions without taking advice.

    autocratic, *adj.*; **autocracy**, *n.*

12. **automaton**   (ô tŏm′ ə tən, ô tŏm′ə tŏn′)   [-*matos* <G. "thinking," "acting"]
    n. A person who behaves in a mechanical, routine manner; a robot.

    Her job on the assembly line caused her to feel like an **automaton.**

13. **autonomy**   (ô tŏn′ə mē)   [*nomos* <G. "law"]
    n. The condition of being self-governing; independence.

    Kenyans fought for **autonomy** from British rule, and Kenya became a republic in 1964.

    autonomous, *adj.*

14. **autopsy**   (ô′ tŏp sē, ô′ təp sē)   [*opsis* <G. "sight." *Autopsy* thus literally means "to see for oneself."]
    n. The examination of a corpse to determine the cause of death.

    An **autopsy** of the mummy revealed that the Pharaoh had died of lead poisoning.

    autopsic, *adj.*; **autopsical**, *adj.*; **autopsis**, *n.*

Familiar Words
egotism

EGO <L. "I"

15. egoism (ē′gō ĭz′ əm)
n. Conceit; valuing everything according to one's personal interest; excessive confidence in the rightness of one's own opinion. (In ethics, egoism is the belief in self-love as a proper motive for human conduct; in psychology, *ego* means "the self," the part of the mind concerned with the outside world.) *Egotism* can mean "boastfulness" and/or "selfishness."

Cleopatra's **egoism** may have resulted from her power, ability, and charm.

egoist, *n.*; **egoistical**, *adj.*

Challenge Words
egocentric
egotistical

EXERCISE 1A   Circle the letter of the best ANTONYM (the word or phrase most nearly opposite the word in bold-faced type).

1. a demonstration of **egoism**   a. self-interest   b. self-improvement   c. religious fervor   d. selflessness   e. virility
2. the attitude of a **misanthrope**   a. person who loves all people   b. person who is less than human   c. miserable person   d. miser   e. hater of all people
3. **humane** attitudes   a. lively   b. compassionate   c. inanimate   d. human   e. cruel
4. **virile** features   a. muscular   b. unmanly   c. rough   d. strongly masculine   e. feminist
5. an issue of **autonomy**   a. dependency   b. income   c. new government   d. self-rule   e. personal identity

Circle the letter of the best SYNONYM (the word or phrase most nearly the same as the word in bold-faced type).

6. research in **gynecology**   a. men's diseases   b. the study of women   c. the accomplishments of women   d. women's health   e. nature conservation
7. answering like a(n) **automaton**   a. robot   b. domineering person   c. autocrat   d. feminist   e. egoist
8. a famous **anthropologist**   a. humanist   b. scientist who studies human origins   c. humanitarian   d. homicide   e. autocrat

9. the suspected **homicide**   a. murder victim   b. robber   c. killer
d. scene of the crime   e. murder weapon
10. influenced by **feminism**   a. feminine behavior   b. women
c. a belief in the equal status of women   d. unmanliness
e. motherhood

EXERCISE 1B   Circle the letter of the sentence in which the word in bold-faced type is used incorrectly.

1. a. The Cabots and the Lowells, proper Bostonians, always
   demonstrated the **humanities** at their afternoon teas.
   b. The sciences are not classified as **humanities.**
   c. The **humanities** courses for freshmen include art and music
   history.
   d. New technology often draws more financial support than do the
   humanities.

2. a. Films of Benito Mussolini rallying fellow Italians during World
   War II reveal his **egoism.**
   b. **Egoists** think of their own interests first.
   c. Napoleon Bonaparte was one of the notable **egoists** in history.
   d. His lifetime career in social work demonstrated his selfless
   egoism.

3. a. The traditional family in China expects the eldest male, usually
   the grandfather, to be **autocratic.**
   b. By dividing power among the legislative, judicial, and executive
   branches of government, the U.S. Constitution prevents a
   president from becoming an **autocrat.**
   c. Children learn to be self-governing by gradual practice in
   autocracy.
   d. Although she officially ruled with her brother, Cleopatra was the
   unquestioned **autocrat** of Roman Egypt.

4. a. Although the police considered the death an act of suicide, Miss
   Marple suspected **homicide** after she attended the investigation.
   b. To prove his theory of "superior men," Raskolnikov became a
   homicide, killing an aged pawnbroker.
   c. Believing his wife Desdemona to be unfaithful, Othello killed her
   in a **homicidal** act of jealousy.
   d. Because the police found five stolen wallets in the pickpocket's
   coat, they charged him with **homicide.**

EXERCISE 1C Fill in each blank with the most appropriate word from Lesson 1. Use a word or any of its forms only once.

1. In recent years many African nations have achieved
   _____autonomy_____ after decades of colonial rule.

2. The office supervisor followed his routine with such mechanical
   consistency that his subordinates called him a(n) _automaton_ .

3. Sir Arthur Conan Doyle assigned his fictional sleuth, Sherlock
   Holmes, to many perplexing cases of _Homicide_ .

4. Until he was transformed by adopting an orphan child, Silas
   Marner was a(n) _____misanthrope_____ who lived in isolation
   and distrusted everyone.

5. Human beings are "the measure of all things" from the point of
   view of _____anthropology_____ .

6. Mary Wollstonecraft, an eighteenth-century _Feminist_ ,
   wrote *A Vindication of the Rights of Woman* in response to Rousseau's
   claim that women's major role was to care for men.

7. Advances in _____gynecology_____ have made it possible for
   women who were once infertile to have children.

8. Because my supervisor is such a(n) _____autocrat_____ , I
   have asked for a transfer to a department in which all employees'
   opinions are valued.

9. Since the Red Cross began inspecting detention camps, prisoners
   of war live in more _____humane_____ conditions.

10. Mikhail Baryshnikov brought new excitement to ballet with his
    _____virile_____ style of dancing.

11. Zora Neale Hurston's studies in _____Humanities_____
    focused on black folklore in the South and in the West Indies.

LESSON 2

Fortuna non mutat genus.
Fortune does not change nature [birth].—HORACE

	Key Words	
congenital	genre	homogeneous
engender	genteel	indigenous
genealogy	gentile	ingenious
genesis	gentry	progenitor
genocide	heterogeneous	progeny

GENOS, GENEOS <G. "race," "family"
GENS, GENTIS <L. "race," "clan," "family"
GENUS, GENERIS <L. "birth," "race," "kind," "tribe," "clan"

1. **genealogy** (jē′nē ŏl′ə jē) [*logos* <G. "word," "speech," "thought"] *n.* A record of descent from one's ancestors; the study of family records.

   Toni Morrison's novel *Song of Solomon* traces the **genealogy** of an American family from the mid-twentieth century back to their African heritage.

   genealogical, *adj.*

2. **genocide** (jĕn′ə sīd) [*occidere* <L. "to kill"] *n.* The planned annihilation of a racial, political, or cultural group.

   The Nazi effort to eliminate all Jews is the most extensive attempt at **genocide** in history.

3. **genre** (zhän′rə) *n.* A type, class, or category, especially of fine art or literature.

   Edna Ferber's writing encompasses several **genres**—fiction, drama, and autobiography.

4. **genteel** (jĕn tēl′) *adj.* Well-mannered; refined; polite. (Sometimes used to mean "falsely polite" or "having affected good manners.")

   Although they tried to look **genteel,** their vulgar language and rude behavior betrayed their lack of refinement.

   gentility, *n.*

5. **gentile** (jĕn′tīl) *n.* Anyone not of the Jewish faith.

   Although they are **gentiles,** they are familiar with Jewish tradition.

6. **gentry** (jĕn′trē) *n.* 1. Aristocratic or well-bred people.

   Their cultivated manners and education showed them to be members of the **gentry.**

   2. In Britain, the class under the aristocracy.

   Several of Jane Austen's novels describe the English **gentry** enjoying their country estates.

   NOTA BENE: A word coined in the twentieth century is *gentrify,* meaning "to upgrade a neighborhood as dwellings and buildings are improved or renovated"; gentrification occurs when middle-class families move into an urban area, causing property values to increase and poorer residents to be forced out.

7. **heterogeneous**   (hĕt′ ər ə jē′ nē əs)   [*heteros* <G. "other"]
adj. Having parts that are unrelated or completely different.

The United States has been called a "melting pot" because of its **heterogeneous** population.

heterogeneity, *n.*

Antonym: **homogeneous**

8. **homogeneous**   (hō mŏj′ ə nəs, hə mŏj′ ə nəs)   [*homos* <G. "same"]
adj. 1. Of the same kind or sort.

As a result of modern weaving technology, thousands of yards of **homogeneous** cloth can be produced by factories in different countries.

2. Composed of parts that are alike.

Because few non-Icelanders live in Iceland, it is a culturally **homogeneous** country.

homogeneity, *n.*; **homogenize**, *v.*; **homogeneously**, *adv.*; **homogeneousness**, *n.*

Antonym: **heterogeneous**

GIGNO, GIGNERE, GENUI, GENITUM <L. "to beget," "to bear," "to bring forth"

Familiar Words
genetic

Challenge Words
primogeniture

9. **congenital**   (kən jĕn′ ə təl)   [*con* = *cum* <L. "with"]
adj. Existing at birth but not hereditary.

The baby is the only member of its family to have a **congenital** heart defect.

10. **engender**   (ĕn jĕn′ dər)   [*en* = *in* <L. "in"]
tr. v. To give rise to; to bring into existence.

The British Parliament's tariff on tea **engendered** violent protests like the Boston Tea Party in the over-taxed American colonies.

11. **genesis**   (jĕn′ ə sĭs)
n. 1. A beginning or origin.

Historians trace the **genesis** of the United Nations to the League of Nations.

2. (capitalized) The first book of the Old Testament.

One story of the creation of the world is told in **Genesis.**

12. **indigenous**   (ĭn dĭj′ə nəs)   [*in* <L. "in"]
adj. 1. Occurring in or characterizing an area; native.

Shinto, a religion **indigenous** to Japan, originated in prehistoric times, while Buddhism was introduced from Korea in the sixth century.

2. Inborn.

Curiosity is a characteristic **indigenous** to human beings.

13. **ingenious**   (ĭ jēn′ yəs)   [*in* <L. "in"]
adj. Cleverly inventive and resourceful.

Harriet Tubman's **ingenious** tactics helped more than 300 slaves escape to freedom.

ingenuity, *n.*; **ingeniousness**, *n.*

NOTA BENE: Do not confuse *ingenious* with *ingenuous* (from *ingenuus* <L. "frankness," "innocence"). *Ingenuous* means "without sophistication or worldliness; innocent," and "frank; naive."

14. **progenitor**   (prō jĕn′ə tər)   [*pro* <L. "before," "for"]
n. A direct ancestor; an originator of a line of descent.

The Wright brothers' flying machine is the **progenitor** of the modern airplane.

15. **progeny**   (prŏj′ə nē)   [*pro* <L. "forth"]
n. Children or descendants; offspring. (Sometimes *progeny* also refers to the results of artistic creativity. For example, Charles Dickens said that of all his progeny—meaning his novels—he loved *David Copperfield* best.)

Most parents take pride in the accomplishments of their **progeny.**

EXERCISE 2A   Circle the letter of the best SYNONYM (the word or phrase most nearly the same as the word in bold-faced type).

1. the infection was **congenital**   a. hereditary   b. troublesome
   c. existent at birth   d. contagious   e. homogeneous
2. to be a **gentile**   a. gentle person   b. well-bred person
   c. non-Jewish person   d. humanist   e. member of a Jewish nation
3. search for one's **genealogy**   a. national history   b. family history
   c. anthropology   d. cultural history   e. personal history
4. characteristics of the **gentry**   a. ancestors   b. progeny
   c. non-Jewish people   d. well-bred people   e. children

Circle the letter of the best ANTONYM (the word or phrase most nearly opposite the word in bold-faced type).

5. the **genesis** of a project   a. category   b. origin   c. founder
   d. end   e. limitations
6. from **heterogeneous** backgrounds   a. married   b. independent
   c. differing   d. similar   e. genteel
7. to **engender** drowsiness   a. pretend   b. put an end to   c. bring
   about   d. expect   e. forbid

EXERCISE 2B   Circle the letter of the sentence in which the word in bold-faced type is used incorrectly.

1. a. His personal library was organized by **genre** and then by author.
   b. A beginning German student learning French may confuse masculine, feminine, and neuter **genres** of nouns.
   c. Dr. Samuel Johnson believed that people most enjoy reading **genres** familiar to them.
   d. The English writer George Eliot chose the novel as the **genre** best suited to her talents.
2. a. In the nineteenth century, wearing a hat and gloves out of doors was a mark of **gentility.**
   b. The actor took speech lessons to acquire a more **genteel** accent.
   c. The murderer showed his **gentility** by quickly confessing to the homicide.
   d. Although they put on **genteel** airs, the Victorian couple lived in poverty.
3. a. The experiment failed because of the **heterogeneity** of the animals being studied.
   b. She was so **heterogeneous** in math that she won every contest.
   c. Despite the **heterogeneous** views of its members, the Senate unanimously approved the new Supreme Court justice.
   d. To assemble a **heterogeneous** freshman class is the aim of many college admissions directors.
4. a. Charles Darwin shocked many devout Victorians when he suggested that some form of ape was the **progenitor** of human beings.
   b. Attending the birthday party were sixty of her **progenitors.**
   c. A Daughter of the American Revolution can prove that one of her **progenitors** fought in the War of American Independence.
   d. Records filed in Salt Lake City help many people find information about their **progenitors.**

5. a. The Seminole are an **indigenous** American people.
   b. Several kinds of rock found on the California coast are not **indigenous** but were brought from different locations by shifting geologic plates.
   c. No matter how hard he tried to earn a living, he remained **indigenous** and dissatisfied.
   d. The potato is **indigenous** to South America.

6. a. Production on an assembly line insures almost perfect **homogeneity** in the cars a factory makes.
   b. Most dairies **homogenize** their milk so that cream does not rise to the top.
   c. After we had **homogenized** the laboratory, no one could detect a trace of the chemical explosion.
   d. Some math teachers prefer **homogeneous** classes so that no student will feel the pace is too slow or too fast.

EXERCISE 2C   Fill in each blank with the most appropriate word from Lesson 2. Use a word or any of its forms only once.

1. All of the doctor's _____progeny_____ have followed their mother's example and have studied medicine too.

2. Throughout history there have been examples of _____Genocide_____ as one group of people finds cause to destroy another.

3. Tom Sawyer's _____ingenious_____ plan convinces his friends to do his work—whitewashing a fence.

4. Designed in 1909, Henry Ford's Model T is the _____Genesis_____ of today's mass-produced automobiles.

5. Students profit from acquiring techniques for reading various _____genres_____: poetry, essays, short stories, and novels.

6. Too much competition can _____engender_____ fear and distrust among students.

7. Although found throughout California, eucalyptus trees are _____Indigenous_____ to Australia.

REVIEW EXERCISES FOR LESSONS 1 AND 2

1 Circle the letter of the best answer to the following questions about roots and definitions.

1. Which Greek or Latin word means the same as *gyne?*
   a. *vir*   b. *genus*   c. *humanus*   d. *femina*   e. *anthropos*

2. Which Greek or Latin word does not belong with the others?
   a. *humanus* b. *auto* c. *anthropos*

3. Which pair of words can accurately be used as synonyms?
   a. progenitor—progeny
   b. egoism—egotism
   c. misogynist—misanthrope
   d. humanism—anthropology

4. Which word is *least* likely to describe an egoist?
   a. autonomous b. ingenious c. humanitarian d. gentile
   e. misanthropic

5. Which of the following explanations of word derivation is incorrect?
   a. *Autocrat* contains the Greek word for "power."
   b. *Misanthrope* contains the Greek word for "man."
   c. *Heterogeneous* contains the Greek word for "other."
   d. *Indigenous* contains the Latin word for "clan."
   e. *Homicide* contains the Latin word for "kill."

2 Substitute the appropriate word from Lessons 1 or 2 for each word or phrase in parentheses in the following paragraphs. No word is used more than once.

1. In nineteenth-century New England, Lyman Beecher was a

  prominent clergyman whose _____ (offspring) shared his liberal thinking on social issues. Two of them were Harriet Beecher Stowe, author of Uncle Tom's Cabin, and the

  minister Henry Ward Beecher, who adhered to _____ (humanitarian) precepts as a supporter of the anti-slavery

  movement and the theory of evolution. A _____ (masculine, dynamic) advocate, Henry Ward Beecher

  _____ (propagated) enthusiasm for the women's suffrage movement.

2. _____ (Scientists) studying the origins of human beings have discovered a remarkable

  _____ (sameness) in the peoples

  _____ (native) to both North and South America. Almost all Native Americans shared not only the same blood type, but also the same immunities. For this reason thousands

  died in what was for the most part a(n) _____ (annihilation) of whole tribes that had no immune defenses to the contagious diseases brought by European invaders.

3 Writing or Discussion Activities

1. You are a travel agent who has been asked to suggest an appropriate summer vacation for each of the following clients. Describe each vacation in a complete sentence that includes the italicized word.
   a. A client with an interest in *genealogy*.
   b. A client with an interest in the *humanities*.
   c. A client with an interest in *indigenous* American art and languages.
   d. A client with an interest in *anthropology*.

2. Select one of the kinds of people listed below and write a monologue from his or her point of view. Have the speaker describe some interest or activity that would be typical of such a person. Let the manner of speaking as well as the topics mentioned reveal what kind of person this is.
   a. A feminist
   b. An autocrat
   c. A misanthrope
   d. An automaton

3. Imagine that you could interview any one of your progenitors about his or her lifetime and experiences. Explain in a paragraph whom you would choose to interview and why. Then list five questions you would like to ask.

LESSONS 3 AND 4

Personal Relationships

LESSON 3

Patris est filius.
He is his father's son
(i.e., a chip off the old block).

Key Words

avuncular	matriarchy	patrimony
bigamy	matriculate	patronage
familial	matrix	patronize
fraternal	monogamy	patronymic
fraternize	patriarch	uxorious

Familiar Words
maternal
maternity
matrimony
matron

MATER, MATRIS <L. "mother"

1. **matrix**   (mā′trĭks)
   n. The surroundings within which something begins or develops.

   Researchers use a **matrix** of nutritious gelatin to grow bacteria in laboratories.

2. **matriarchy**   (mā′trē är′kē)   [*archy* <G. *arkhein*, "to rule"]
n. A society ruled or controlled by women.

Anthropological research suggests that the early society of Crete was a **matriarchy.**

matriarch, *n.*; **matriarchal**, *adj.*

3. **matriculate**   (mə trĭk′ yə lāt)

tr. and *intr. v.* To register as a student at a college or university.

Oberlin was the first American college to allow both women and men to **matriculate.**

matriculation, *n.*

PATER, PATRIS <L. "father"

4. **patriarch**   (pā′trē ärk)   [*arch* <G. *arkhein*, "to rule"]
n. 1. The male head of a family or tribe.

The **patriarch** was honored as the chief historian of the tribe.

2. An Old Testament ancestor.

Jacob was the **patriarch** of the twelve tribes of Israel.

3. A founding father or wise man.

Americans look upon George Washington as their **patriarch.**

patriarchal, *adj.*; **patriarchy**, *n.*

5. **patrimony**   (păt′ rə mō′ nē)
n. A family inheritance.

Islamic law allows a woman to retain all rights to her **patrimony** when she marries.

patrimonial, *adj.*

6. **patronage**   (pā′trə nĭj, păt′ rə nĭj)
n. 1. Support; encouragement.

Political contenders vie for the **patronage** of wealthy citizens.

2. Business clientele; customers.

Because of its efficiency and courtesy the new bank has attracted the **patronage** of many business people.

7. **patronize** (pa′trə nīz, pat′rə nīz)
tr. v. 1. To go to regularly.

We **patronize** the local grocery store.

2. To treat someone as an inferior.

"Don't **patronize** me," the patient said when the doctor dismissed her questions.

patronizing, *adj.*

8. **patronymic** (păt′rə nĭm′ĭk) [*nym* <G. *onoma,* "name"]
n. Name derived from a paternal ancestor.

Peterson is the **patronymic** of *Peter's son.*

Familiar Words
fraternity

FRATER, FRATRIS <L. "brother"

9. **fraternal** (frə tûr′nəl)
adj. Pertaining to brothers; brotherly.

Although separated for many years, the brothers still retained a fierce **fraternal** loyalty.

Challenge Words
confrere
fratricide

10. **fraternize** (frăt′ ər nīz)
intr. v. 1. To be friendly with.

The new teacher soon **fraternized** easily with her colleagues.

2. To socialize with an enemy population.

Warning the troops not to **fraternize,** the commander declared off limits all taverns and restaurants in the occupied town.

fraternization, *n.*

AVUNCULUS, AVUNCULI <L. "uncle"

11. **avuncular** (ə vŭng′ kyə lər)
adj. Like an uncle.

We appreciated his **avuncular** gestures like trips to the ball park and treats of ice cream.

Familiar Words
familiar
family

FAMILIA <L. "family"

12. **familial** (fə mĭl′yəl)
adj. Having to do with the family.

One branch of anthropology studies **familial** structures in different cultures.

UXOR, UXORIS <L. "wife"

13. **uxorious**   (ŭk′ sôr′ ē əs, ŭk′ sōr′ ē əs)
    adj. Dominated by one's wife.

    The **uxorious** husband catered to his wife's every whim.

GAMOS <G. "marriage"

14. **bigamy**   (bĭg′ ə mē)   [*bi* <G. "two"]
    n. Marriage to two mates.

    Mr. Rochester would have committed **bigamy** if he had married Jane Eyre while his wife was still alive.

    bigamist, *n.*; **bigamous**, *adj.*

15. **monogamy**   (mə nŏg′ ə mē)   [*monos* <G. "alone"]
    n. Marriage to a single mate.

    The Constitution recognizes **monogamy** as the only legal form of marriage in the United States.

    monogamist, *n.*; **monogamous**, *adj.*

EXERCISE 3A

Circle the letter of the best ANTONYM (the word or phrase most nearly opposite the word(s) in bold-faced type).

1. their **patronage of** the arts   a. support for   b. opposition to
   c. advertisement of   d. festival of   e. interest in
2. to **fraternize** with the enemies   a. trade   b. talk   c. refuse to socialize   d. become brothers   e. make peace
3. the **uxorious** husband   a. overbearing   b. supportive   c. humane
   d. monogamous   e. unfaithful
4. a **patronizing** remark   a. familiar   b. flattering   c. scornful
   d. charming   e. misanthropic

Circle the letter of the best SYNONYM (the word or phrase most nearly the same as the word in bold-faced type).

5. hatched in a high-protein **matrix**   a. environment   b. bottle
   c. substitute   d. progeny   e. gas
6. the **patriarch** of the village   a. leader   b. progenitor
   c. patriot   d. teacher   e. patron
7. anticipated their **matriculation**   a. grades   b. suspension
   c. awards   d. enrollment   e. arrival

EXERCISE 3B   Circle the letter of the sentence in which the word in bold-faced type is used incorrectly.

1. a. Isabel Archer receives from an uncle a large **patrimony** that enables her to live and travel independently.
   b. After paying their father's debts, no **patrimony** remained for the brothers.
   c. The crew gave a **patrimonial** dinner to honor their retiring leader.
   d. As the only heir, Eleanor of Aquitaine received a **patrimony** surpassing many kingdoms.

2. a. A precocious student, she **matriculated** at the university when she was fifteen.
   b. Water can be purified by **matriculation** through a series of filters.
   c. You cannot check out books from the college library until you have **matriculated.**
   d. Because of his illness during the autumn, he postponed **matriculating** until the second semester.

3. a. Although Elizabeth I of England had many suitors, she never married, and remained a **monogamist** all her life.
   b. Unlike the swan, who keeps one mate for life, most animals are not **monogamous.**
   c. "Serial **monogamy**" is having several mates but one at a time.
   d. Although divorce was easily and frequently obtained, ancient Roman society was **monogamous.**

4. a. At Thanksgiving we all visit Grandma, the family **matriarch.**
   b. I could imagine an energetic woman like her as a leader in a **matriarchy.**
   c. Although men held the positions of leadership, the tribe was considered **matriarchal** because women controlled all property.
   d. Catherine the Great rode to her coronation in a gilded **matriarch.**

5. a. The **familial** tune reminded us of college football games.
   b. She shared with her brothers the **familial** trait of cheerfulness.
   c. Although a demanding executive, in **familial** matters she is patient and accepting.
   d. Few strangers are privileged to enter Spanish **familial** circles.

6. a. The **bigamist** was prosecuted when both his wives filed suit against him.
   b. In Tibet **bigamy** is allowed only when a man marries his brother's widow.
   c. According to a new Marriage Law, **bigamy** was prohibited.
   d. Before they stood upright, **bigamists** moved on four legs.

7. a. The crystals were found in a granite **matrix.**

     b. The diverse cultural **matrix** of Constantinople, situated between Europe and Asia, gave rise to a new architectural style that combined both influences.

     c. Some anthropologists believe that the **matrix** of human evolution was East Africa.

     d. Only a strong **matrix** like Aunt Martha could have held the family together.

8. a. *Lavransdatter* is a Norwegian **patronymic** that means "the daughter of Lavran."

     b. Names like Fitzpatrick and Fitzgerald are **patronymics** derived from the French word *fils,* which means "son."

     c. She squandered her entire **patronymic** on the stock market.

     d. Russian names include a first name, a **patronymic**, and a family name.

9. a. **Fraternize** yourself with the rules before you attempt to play chess.

     b. The faculty seldom **fraternized** with the students.

     c. During World War II the French underground gained military information by **fraternizing** with German soldiers.

     d. All the tourist's efforts to **fraternize** with the villagers ended in rejection.

10. a. We seldom **patronize** this store because the clerks are very rude.

     b. The seniors have a **patronizing** attitude toward all freshmen.

     c. If you can't **patronize** this candidate's views, don't support her.

     d. She never **patronizes** restaurants where smoking is permitted.

11. a. He was insulted by her **patronage**, especially her references to his "low origins."

     b. Public television stations depend financially on the **patronage** of the viewers.

     c. Upon retirement, Dr. Wong sold both her office and **patronage** to a young dentist.

     d. The **patronage** of the Mellon family has enabled the art museum to make major purchases.

12. a. He took an **avuncular** interest in the neighbor's children.

     b. An **avuncular** infection can cause deafness.

     c. **Avuncular** affection led him to make his niece his heir.

     d. Letting me stay up late and eat lots of chocolate were **avuncular** indulgences both my uncle and I enjoyed.

EXERCISE 3C

Fill in each blank with the most appropriate word from Lesson 3. Use a word or any of its forms only once.

1. Walter Mitty was so ___uxorious___ that he couldn't buy puppy biscuits without consulting his wife.

2. Although they were not wealthy, her parents left her a rich
   ___Patrimony___ by giving her a fine education.
3. Showing us photographs from her childhood, Grandmother
   pointed out the distinctive ___familial___ resemblance among
   her cousins.
4. After Uncle Nick died, I realized how much I depended on his
   ___avuncular___ affection.
5. In the movie, the deceitful ___bigamist___ maintained a wife, two
   children, and a dog in two different cities.
6. Although permitted several wives by Chinese law, the emperor
   chose to remain ___monogamist___ out of devotion to his first wife.
7. Although unrelated, the foster brothers developed a strong
   ___fraternal___ bond.

LESSON 4

De mortuis nil nisi bonum.
[Say] nothing about the dead but good.—TRADITIONAL

	Key Words	
entity	mortify	pedagogue
essence	naive	pedant
euthanasia	nascent	postmortem
innate	nonentity	puerile
moribund	orthopedics	renaissance

PUER <L. "a male child"

1. **puerile**   (py$\overline{oo}$′ər ĭl, py$\overline{oo}$′ĭl, pwĕr′ĭl)
   adj. Childish; immature.

   Forced to take my little sister to the party, I was humiliated by her **puerile**
   giggling.

Familiar Words
encyclopedia
pediatrics

PAIS, PAIDOS <G. "child," "boy"

2. orthopedics   (ôr′ thə pē′ dĭks)   [*ortho* <G. "straight," "correct"]
n. Branch of medicine treating disorders of the skeletal system and
tissues related to movement.

The specialist in **orthopedics** set my broken leg.

orthopedic, *adj.*; **orthopedist**, *n.*

3. pedagogue   (pĕd′ ə gŏg′, pĕd′ ə gôg′)   [*gogue* <G. *agogos*,
"leader"]
n. A teacher.

The Oxford Cleric in Chaucer's *Canterbury Tales* is a devoted **pedagogue** who would "gladly . . . learn and gladly teach."

pedagogic, *adj.*; **pedagogical**, *adj.*; **pedagogy**, *n.*

4. pedant   (pĕd′ ənt)
n. 1. A person who pays excessive attention
to learning rules rather than to
understanding.

A true scholar seeks to understand the causes
of historical events, but a **pedant** only
memorizes their dates.

2. A scholarly show-off.

Instead of saying "horse," the **pedant** Mr. Bounderby in Charles Dick-
en's *Hard Times* refers to a "granivorous quadruped."

pedantic, *adj.*; **pedantry**, *n.*

Familiar Words
absent
essential
future
present
presentation
represent

SUM, ESSE, FUI, FUTURUM <L. "to be"

5. entity   (ĕn′ tə tē)
n. Something that has a real or independent existence.

Each twin wanted to be treated as an **entity.**

Antonym: **nonentity**

6. nonentity   (nŏn ĕn′ tə tē)
n. 1. A person or thing of no importance.

How did such a **nonentity** achieve so much power?

  2. Something that does not exist or exists only in the imagination.

Challenge Words
in absentia
quintessential

Although a monster in a nightmare is a **nonentity,** it can cause real fear.

Antonym: **entity**

7. **essence**   (ĕs′ əns)

   n. 1. The basic element; the identifying characteristic.

   During the 1920s Bessie Smith's singing represented the **essence** of the blues.

   2. A substance in concentrated form obtained from a plant or drug.

   Ground seeds of the cacao bean are the **essence** of cocoa.

   3. A perfume.

   The delicate **essence** of lavender scented the room.

   (*Quintessence* means "an even purer, more concentrated form" or "a perfect embodiment of something.")

Familiar Words
immortal
mortal
mortgage
mortician
mortuary

Challenge Words
amortize
rigor mortis

MORIOR, MORI, MORTUUM <L. "to die"

8. **moribund**   (môr′ ə bŭnd, mŏr′ ə bŭnd)

   adj. About to die or end.

   As automobiles became popular, the speed limits set for horse-drawn vehicles became **moribund.**

   moribundity, *n.*

9. **mortify**   (môr′ tə fī)   [*-fy = facere* <L. "to make"]

   tr. v. 1. To shame.

   In *Pride and Prejudice,* Mrs. Bennet's crude efforts to marry off her five daughters **mortify** Elizabeth Bennet.

   2. To discipline oneself by denial.

   Some Hindus seek to **mortify** the flesh by prolonged fasting.

   mortification, *n.*

10. **postmortem**   (pōst môr′ təm)   [*post* <L. "after"]

    n. 1. An examination to determine the cause of death; an autopsy.

    The **postmortem** eliminated the possibility of death by poison.

    2. (informal) An analysis of something that is over.

    Every Monday at lunch there is a **postmortem** of Sunday's baseball game.

THANATOS <G. "death"

11. euthanasia (yōō′ thə nā′ zhə, yōō′ thə nā′ shə) [*eu* <G. "well"]
n. The act of painlessly killing a suffering person or animal; mercy killing.

Controversy continues over a patient's right to **euthanasia.**

NASCOR, NASCI, NATUM <L. "to be born"

Familiar Words
natal
nation
native
nature
noel
prenatal

Challenge Words
cognate
nee
neonatal
renascence

12. innate (ĭ nāt′, ĭn′ āt) [*in* <L. "in"]
adj. Possessed at birth; inborn.

Voice lessons have improved his **innate** singing talent.

innately, *adv.*

13. naive (nä ēv′)
adj. 1. Childlike; unsophisticated.

She retained a **naive** belief that her toys came alive by night.

2. Gullible.

The **naive** tourists bought "ancient coins" from dishonest street vendors.

naivete, *n.*

14. nascent (năs′ənt, nā′sənt)
adj. Emerging; coming into existence.

Good teachers encourage the **nascent** skills of young writers.

15. renaissance (rĕn′ ə säns′, rĕn′ ə zäns′) [*re* <L. "back," "again"]
n. 1. A rebirth; a renewal.

The twentieth century has witnessed a **renaissance** of interest in indigenous American art.

2. (capitalized) A revival of humanism in fourteenth-century to sixteenth-century Europe.

During the **Renaissance** the humanities were greatly influenced by Greek and Roman models.

EXERCISE 4A   Circle the letter of the best ANTONYM (the word or phrase most nearly opposite the word in bold-faced type).

1. their **puerile** choice   a. mature   b. innocent   c. girlish   d. pearllike   e. avuncular

2. our hopes were **moribund**   a. nascent   b. boundless   c. foolish
    d. naive   e. arrested

3. a **naive** remark   a. silly   b. dishonest   c. strange   d. rude
    e. sophisticated

4. intentionally chose a(n) **nonentity**   a. important person
    b. pedant   c. basic element   d. careless person   e. mature person

5. a **renaissance** in bluegrass music   a. pedagogue   b. genesis
    c. decline   d. patrimony   e. progeny

Circle the letter of the best SYNONYM (the word or phrase most nearly the same as the word in bold-faced type).

6. this **innate** quality   a. hereditary   b. secret   c. destructive
    d. boring   e. nascent

7. **mortifying** situations   a. funny   b. expensive   c. fatal
    d. moribund   e. painfully embarrassing

8. recognized your **nascent** talent   a. decent   b. athletic   c. familial
    d. immortal   e. budding

9. became increasingly **pedantic**   a. interested in shoes   b. evil
    c. humiliating   d. witty   e. foolishly attentive to detail

10. **pedagogic** success   a. educational   b. mathematical
    c. medical   d. immature   e. essential

EXERCISE 4B

Circle the letter of the sentence in which the word in bold-faced type is used incorrectly.

1. a. **Pedants** have the right-of-way at intersections.
    b. Only a **pedant** would be so picky about footnotes in a personal letter.
    c. Despite his occasional **pedantry** he is a teacher beloved by his students.
    d. Her **pedantic** lecture on carbon dating destroyed my interest in archaeology.

2. a. **Orthopedic** shoes can help correct a child's club foot.
    b. An **orthopedist** at a ski resort has a large practice during the winter.
    c. Help! There's a green **orthopede** in my sleeping bag.
    d. Modern **orthopedics** can improve most curvatures of the spine.

3. a. Our plans to remodel the house have become **moribund** since the economic recession.
    b. Because of competition from the airlines, many railroads are now **moribund.**

    c. He wore a plaid **moribund** with his tuxedo.

    d. Hypochondriacs think they're **moribund** when they have only have a cold.

4. a. However good the intentions, **euthanasia** is extremely controversial.

    b. The lawyer's strong statement supporting **euthanasia** won the sympathy of the jury.

    c. Her **euthanasia** for sailing led to a year-long yachting trip.

    d. The debating team chose the topic "Resolved: **Euthanasia** should be permitted in cases of terminal disease."

5. a. Only someone **nascent** to the United States may run for president.

    b. Her teacher encouraged her **nascent** interest in Mayan culture.

    c. Political analysts observed a **nascent** radicalism among rural voters.

    d. Their **nascent** sense of independence was frustrated by the school's rigid rules.

6. a. His **innate** tact and consideration make him an excellent diplomat.

    b. Cats **innately** hate water.

    c. The ability to speak is **innate** in human beings.

    d. When she received the bill, she was so **innate** that she threatened to sue.

7. a. Our English teacher used odd **pedagogic** techniques like wearing funny hats and singing rules for punctuation to keep our attention.

    b. Jan was a child **pedagogue**, playing with the Vienna Philharmonic at age twelve.

    c. Education courses stress effective **pedagogy.**

    d. Lecturing is still common **pedagogical** practice at the university level.

8. a. This new perfume is called "**Essence** of Violets."

    b. His frequent travel and fluency in many languages make him the **essence** of worldliness.

    c. Some people are born with limited **essences** of smell.

    d. Claude Brown's autobiography captures the **essence** of Harlem in the 1940s and 1950s.

9. a. He had an **entity** for exotic foods.

    b. Hard work and concern for constituents turned the senator into an influential political **entity.**

    c. Although she began her career with a large firm, she later went into business for herself as a separate **entity.**

    d. Although certain phenomena have no physical **entity**, scientific instruments can prove their existence.

EXERCISE 4C   Fill in each blank with the most appropriate word from Lesson 4. Use a
word or any of its forms only once.

1. Refusing to let boos from the balcony _____
   her, the composer made a dignified bow after the world premiere
   of her symphony.

2. The health department ordered a(n) _____
   to determine whether the dead dog had rabies.

3. Anyone with such_____ behavior cannot be
   given a responsible job.

4. The _____ brace relieved the pain from his
   neck injury.

5. My city cousins were so _____ about
   backpacking that they brought along a hairdryer and a tapedeck.

6. He is _____ to insist that we say "I shall"
   instead of "I will."

REVIEW EXERCISES FOR LESSONS 3 AND 4

1 Circle the letter of the best answer to the following analogies and questions
about roots and definitions.

1. *mater* : *pater* : :
   a. paternal : maternal
   b. puerile : naive
   c. *frater* : *avunculus*
   d. patrimony : matrimony
   e. matriarch : patriarch
2. *morior* : *nascor* : :
   a. to die ; *thanatos*
   b. pendant : pedagogue
   c. mortify : fortify
   d. *puer* : *pais*
   e. moribund : nascent
3. patronize : *pater* : :
   a. pedagogue : teacher
   b. postmortem : autopsy
   c. fraternal : *frater*
   d. *thanatos* : euthanasia
   e. *esse* : essential

4. bigamy : monogamy : :
   a. entity : nonentity
   b. nonentity : essence
   c. patricide : suicide
   d. 2 : 1
   e. divorce : annulment
5. Which root does *not* refer to a family relationship?
   a. *uxor* b. *frater* c. *avunculus* d. *puer* e. *pater*

2 Substitute the appropriate word from Lessons 3 or 4 for each word or phrase in parentheses in the following paragraphs. No word is used more than once.

1. Until the nineteenth century, most Europeans were educated in a

   manner that dated back to the _____
   (rebirth) of humanism in the late Middle Ages. However, the basis

   of this _____ (method of teaching), the
   study of Greek and Latin literature, proved impractical in the

   _____ (emerging) colonial empires. To work,
   engage in trade, and relate on friendly terms with people in other
   parts of the world, Europeans needed to study foreign languages,
   geography, science, and mathematics. Because these educational
   reforms have prevailed, the study of Greek and Latin is today

   _____ (about to die out).

2. English Queen Victoria is renowned as a _____
   (a powerful female ruler) for her longevity on the throne as well as

   her _____ (family-minded) role as mother of
   eight children born between 1840 and 1867. However, her consort

   and husband, Prince Albert, was not _____
   (dominated by his wife). He possessed independence and generosity;

   historians cite him for his _____ (inborn)
   good judgment when in 1861 he served a diplomatic role that
   deflected war between England and the United States.

3 Writing or Discussion Activities

1. Write a brief dialogue that illustrates the way the kinds of people
   described below would speak and respond in the given situation.
   a. An uxorious husband and his dominating wife order dinner in a
      restaurant.
   b. A pedantic pedagogue has a conference with a puerile student to
      discuss the student's work.

2. Several words in Lessons 3 and 4 have more than one meaning. Write two sentences that illustrate different meanings of each of the following words.
   a. patriarch
   b. patronage
   c. essence
   d. mortify

3. Do you know someone whose family name is a patronymic? Make a list of the people whom you know with patronymic names. Use at least one of these patronymic names in a sentence. (Suggestion: If you don't know someone, check your school roster or a telephone book.)

LESSONS 5 AND 6

Feelings

LESSON 5

Amor vincit omnia.
Love conquers all.—VIRGIL, *Eclogues X, 69*

Key Words		
acrophobia	enamored	pacify
amicable	hydrophobia	philanthropy
amity	inimical	phobia
appease	odious	xenophobia
bibliophile	pacific	

Familiar Words
amateur
amiable
amorous
enemy

AMO, AMARE, AMAVI, AMATUM <L. "to love"
AMICUS <L. "friend"

1. **amicable**   (ăm′ĭ kə bəl)
   adj. Friendly; peaceable.

   An **amicable** settlement of the dispute prevented ill feelings.

   amicability, *n.*; **amicableness**, *n.*; **amicably**, *adv.*

2. **amity**   (ăm′ə tē)
   n. Friendship; friendly relations.

   Amity has long existed between the United States and Canada.

3. **enamored**   (ĭ năm′rd)   [*en* = *in* <L. "in"]
adj. In love with; charmed by (used with *of*).

They were so **enamored** of Islamic art that they extended their stay in Turkey.

4. **inimical**   (ĭn ĭm′ ĭ kəl)   [*in* <L. "not"]
adj. 1. Harmful.

Too much caffeine is **inimical** to your health.

2. Hostile; unfriendly.

Despite the parents' efforts to reconcile their progeny, the sisters' relationship remained **inimical.**

ODIUM <L. "hate"

5. **odious**   (o′dē əs)
adj. Hateful; distasteful.

Charlotte Brontë's description of the **odious** Lowood School in *Jane Eyre* was drawn from her own experience with inhumane teachers at boarding school.

odiously, *adv.*; **odiousness,** *n.*; **odium,** *n.*

PHILOS <G. "friend"
PHILEO, PHILEIN <G. "to love"

6. **bibliophile**   (bĭb′ lē ə fīl)   [*biblios* <G. "book"]
n. A lover of books.

A visit to the Library of Congress in Washington, D.C., was the highlight of the trip for the **bibliophile.**

bibliophilia, *n.*

7. **philanthropy**   (fĭ lăn′ thrə pē)   [*anthropos* <G. "man"]
n. 1. Goodwill to fellow human beings.

The leaders felt a spirit of **philanthropy** at the signing of the peace treaty.

2. A charitable gift, act, or organization.

Andrew Carnegie's **philanthropy** provided for public libraries throughout the United States.

philanthropic, *adj.*; **philanthropical**, *adj.*; **philanthropist**, *n.*
Antonym: **misanthropy**

PHOBOS <G. "fear," "flight"

8. **phobia** (fō′ bē ə)
    n. Strong, irrational fear.

    Her **phobia** of enclosed spaces prevents her from riding in elevators or automobiles.

    phobic, *adj.*

9. **acrophobia** (ăk′ rə fō′ bē ə) [*acros* <G. "at the farthest point" (usually referring to height)]
    n. Fear of heights.

    Acrophobia prevented my climbing to the top of the tower.

    acrophobe, *n.*

10. **hydrophobia** (hī′ drə fō′ bē ə) [*hydros* <G. "water"]
     n. 1. Fear of water.

     Despite his **hydrophobia,** he finally learned to swim.

     2. Rabies (a usually fatal disease caused by a bite from an infected animal).

     The child who was bitten by a sick squirrel received antirabies vaccine to combat **hydrophobia.**

     hydrophobe, *n.*

11. **xenophobia** (zĕn ə fō′ bē ə) [*xenos* <G. "stranger"]
     n. Fear or hatred of what is strange or foreign, or of foreigners.

     In 2001, the UN's Conference against Racism, Racial Discrimination, **Xenophobia**, and Intolerance was held in South Africa.

     xenophobe, *n.*

PAX, PACIS <L. "peace"

12. **appease** (ə pēz′) [*ap* = *ad* <L. "to," "toward"]
     tr. v. To calm; to satisfy by making concessions or giving into demands.

The prime minister **appeased** the angry crowd by promises of early elections.

appeasable, *adj.*; **appeasably**, *adv.*; **appeasement**, *n.*; **appeaser**, *n.*

13. **pacific** (pə sĭf′ ĭk)
adj. Peaceful; serene.

Because the newly discovered ocean seemed so peaceful, Ferdinand Magellan called it "The **Pacific.**"

pacifically, *adv.*

14. **pacify** (păs′ ə fī)
tr. v. 1. To calm; to make quiet.

Finding the lost doll appeared to be the only way to **pacify** the sobbing child.

2. To end war or violence.

In 1485 the feuding houses of York and Lancaster were finally **pacified,** and the Wars of the Roses concluded when Henry of Lancaster married Elizabeth of York.

pacifiable, *adj.*; **pacificate**, *v.*; **pacification**, *n.*; **pacifier**, *n.*; **pacifism**, *n.*; **pacifist**, *n.*

EXERCISE 5A

Circle the letter of the best SYNONYM (the word or phrase most nearly the same as the word(s) in bold-faced type).

1. to suffer from **hydrophobia**   a. rabies   b. fear of heights   c. fear of cats   d. fear of enclosure   e. drought
2. a(n) **phobia about** dogs   a. fascination with   b. dream of   c. fantasy about   d. fear of   e. interest in
3. a policy of **appeasement**   a. autonomy   b. agitation   c. amity   d. xenophobia   e. euthanasia
4. to be **enamored of** a novel   a. insulted by   b. bored with   c. annoyed with   d. in love with   e. defensive about

Circle the letter of the best ANTONYM (the word or phrase most nearly opposite the word in bold-faced type).

5. the jury's **inimical** verdict   a. incomparable   b. imitative   c. hostile   d. friendly   e. pitiless
6. the **odious** duty   a. long-expected   b. fateful   c. hateful   d. desirable   e. necessary

7. their deeply felt **philanthropy**   a. support of a charity
    b. amicability   c. curiosity   d. dislike of people   e. pride
8. an unapologetic **xenophobe**   a. disciplinarian   b. judge
    c. critic   d. appreciator of new things   e. philanthropist
9. a(n) instinctive **amity**   a. autonomy   b. phobia   c. dislike
    d. appeasement   e. mortification

EXERCISE 5B   Circle the letter of the sentence in which the word in bold-faced type is used incorrectly.

1. a. A true **bibliophile** cannot pass a bookstore without stopping.
    b. Many reputations were ruined when Mata Hari, a spy for
       Germany during World War I, began to write her **bibliophile.**
    c. The extent of her **bibliophilia** became evident when she brought
       a whole suitcase of books on the trip.
    d. No **bibliophile** would leave a book open in the sun this way.
2. a. However polite, relations between Queen Victoria and the
       British prime minister William Gladstone were never **amicable.**
    b. Only your best **amicables** will tell you!
    c. **Amicable** feelings among neighbors led to an annual Labor Day
       block party.
    d. The timber wolf wagged its tail **amicably.**
3. a. Her **acrophobia** worsened in the open squares of Paris.
    b. Because of his **acrophobia**, he refused to go to the top of the
       Empire State Building.
    c. A rock climber cannot be subject to **acrophobia.**
    d. A sudden attack of **acrophobia** made the roofer cling to the
       ladder in terror.
4. a. The frustrated babysitter managed to **pacify** the cranky baby with
       an extra bottle.
    b. Because they could neither conquer nor **pacify** the Scots, the
       Romans built a wall across northern England to keep the Scots
       out of Britain.
    c. The Treaty of Versailles attempted to insure the **pacification** of
       Europe by totally disarming Germany after World War I.
    d. Please **pacify** your complaint in writing to the manager.

EXERCISE 5C   Fill in each blank with the most appropriate word from Lesson 5. Use a word or any of its forms only once.

1. A long history of territorial conflicts has made Greeks and Turks ___*odious*___ toward each other.

2. The government has encouraged ___*philanthropy*___ by making charitable contributions tax deductible.

3. Her fear of disease has made her ___*phobic*___ about germs.

4. Like a true ___*bibliophile*___, she asked to see the library first.

5. The ___*pacific*___ woodland glade was disrupted by the noise of a motorcycle club racing through.

6. She became so ___*enamored*___ of Venice after a summer there that she changed her major to Italian.

7. Uriah Heep's pretense of being humble when he is, in fact, arrogant and sneaky, makes him a(n) ___*odious*___ character in *David Copperfield*.

8. Although not close friends, we have maintained ___*amicable*___ relations with our next-door neighbors for a decade.

9. When the director angrily threatened to recast the play with more diligent students, we tried to ___*appease*___ her by promising to help build sets and make costumes.

10. In his struggle against racial injustice, Martin Luther King, Jr., used nonviolent resistance, a form of ___*pacification*___ he learned from Mahatma Gandhi.

LESSON 6

Radix omnium malorum est cupiditas.
The love of money is the root of all evil.—EPISTLE OF TIMOTHY

Key Words		
antipathy	dysentery	misogyny
apathy	dyslexia	pathological
complacent	empathy	pathos
covet	implacable	placate
cupidity	misogamy	placid

PATHOS <G. "suffering"

1. **antipathy**   (ăn tĭp′ ə thē)   [*anti* <G. "against"]
   n. A hatred or dislike.

   Henry David Thoreau's **antipathy** toward slavery led him to deliver speeches supporting the abolitionist movement.

   antipathetic, *adj.*; **antipathetical**, *adj.*; **antipathetically**, *adv.*

2. **apathy**   (ăp′ ə thē)   [*a* <G. "not," "without"]
   n. 1. Lack of feeling, energy, or interest.

   Because they have not provided enough low-income housing, city governments have been accused of **apathy** toward the homeless.

   2. Indifference.

   That only ten percent of citizens voted reflects widespread **apathy** toward politics.

   apathetic, *adj.*

3. **empathy**   (ĕm′ pə thē)   [*em = in* <L. "in"]
   n. The ability to identify with someone else and understand that person's situation of feelings.

   Her **empathy** for the loneliness of the elderly made her an ideal counselor for the nursing home.

   empathic, *adj.*; **empathically**, *adv.*; **empathize**, *v.*

4. **pathological**   (păth′ ə lŏj′ ĭ kəl)   [*logos* <G. "word," "speech," "thought"]
   adj. 1. Referring to pathology, the study of disease.

   Recent **pathological** research shows that the "common cold" is not caused by a single virus but by a combination of different viruses.

   2. Caused by disease.

   The child's lack of energy was not due to laziness but had **pathological** causes.

   3. Abnormal in behavior.

   Although she owned real diamonds, the heiress had a **pathological** need to shoplift cheap jewelry.

   pathologic, *adj.*; **pathology**, *n.*; **pathologist**, *n.*

5. **pathos**   (pă′ thŏs, pā′ thôs)
   n. A feeling of sympathy; a quality that arouses pity or tenderness.

In a scene of great **pathos,** King Lear laments the death of his faithful daughter, Cordelia.

MISO, MISEIN <G. "to hate"

6. **misogamy** (mĭˈsŏgˈə mē) [*gamos* <G. "marriage"]
   n. Hatred of marriage.

   Her **misogamy** may have its origins in her parents' unhappy marriage.

   misogamist, *n.*; **misogamistic,** *adj.*

7. **misogyny** (mə sŏjˈə nē) [*gyne* <G. "woman"]
   n. Hatred of women.

   Eliza Doolittle's innate charm and intelligence help overcome Professor Henry Higgins's **misogyny** in *My Fair Lady.*

   misogynic, *adj.*; **misogynist,** *n.*; **misogynistic,** *adj.*; **misogynous,** *adj.*

   NOTA BENE: Many English words begin with *mis* <Middle English meaning "wrong" (e.g., *misconduct, misfortune,* and *misunderstanding*). If you recognize a complete English word after *mis* (e.g., *conduct, fortune,* or *understand*), it usually means "wrong." If you do not recognize a complete English word after *mis* (e.g., *gamy* or *gyny*), it probably means "to hate."

DYS <G. "diseased," "difficult," "faulty," "bad"

8. **dysentery** (dĭsˈən tĕr ē)
   n. Severe diarrhea.

   After drinking from the village well, the travelers suffered **dysentery.**

9. **dyslexia** (dĭs lĕkˈse ə) [*lexis* <G. "speech"]
   n. A specific learning disability that is neurological in origin. It is a deficit in the phonological component of language and is characterized by poor spelling and decoding abilities.

   Dyslexia is a common cause of reading, spelling, and writing difficulties.

   dyslexic, *adj.*

CUPIO, CUPERE, CUPIVI, CUPIDUM <L. "to desire"

10. **covet** (kŭvˈĭt)
    tr. v. To crave or desire, especially something belonging to someone else.

Because he **coveted** the throne of England, Richard of Gloucester murdered his nephews, the rightful heirs.

coveted, *adj.*; **covetous**, *adj.*; **covetously**, *adv.*; **covetousness**, *n.*

11. **cupidity**   (kyōō pĭd′ ə tē)
    n. Greed; avarice.

    A father in Balzac's *Pere Goriot* sacrifices himself to satisfy his daughter's **cupidity** for money and power.

PLACEO, PLACERE, PLACUI, PLACITUM <L. "to please"
PLACO, PLACARE, PLACAVI, PLACATUM <L. "to soothe"

12. **complacent**   (kəm plā′sənt)   [*com* <L. intensifier]
    adj. Self-satisfied; smug.

    Complacent in their wealth, the eighteenth-century French aristocracy remained unaware of the plight of the poor.

    complacence, *n.*; **complacency**, *n.*; **complacently**, *adv.*

    NOTA BENE: Make a distinction between *complacent* and *complaisant*, which means "eager to do what pleases others."

13. **implacable** (ĭm plā′kə bəl, ĭm plăk′ ə bəl)   [*im* = *in* <L. "not"]
    adj. Impossible to calm or appease.

    Although often imprisoned, Emmeline Pankhurst was an **implacable** crusader for women's right to vote in England.

    Antonym: **placable**
    implacability, *n.*; **implacableness**, *n.*

14. **placate**   (plā′kāt)
    tr. v. To calm; to pacify; to appease.

    Galileo tried to **placate** the Catholic church in Rome by retracting his theory that the earth revolved around the sun.

    placater, *n.*; **placation**, *n.*; **placatory**, *adj.*; **placative**, *adj.*

15. **placid**   (plăs′ĭd)
    adj. Showing calmness, peacefulness, or composure.

    The usually **placid** bay churned as the hurricane approached.

    placidity, *n.*; **placidness**, *n.*; **placidly**, *adv.*

EXERCISE 6A   Circle the letter of the best SYNONYM (the word or phrase most nearly the same as the word in bold-faced type).

1. a **placid** river   a. sluggish   b. polluted   c. peaceful   d. pathetic
   e. raging
2. a stirring of **pathos**   a. pity   b. harmony   c. amity   d. distrust
   e. fear
3. no **empathy for** acrophobics   a. sympathy for   b. amity with
   c. curiosity about   d. identification with   e. patronage for
4. their **complacent** attitude   a. apathetic   b. empathetic   c. smug
   d. odious   e. phobic

Circle the letter of the best ANTONYM (the word or phrase most nearly opposite the word in bold-faced type).

5. a sudden **antipathy**   a. dislike   b. illness   c. snack   d. loathing
   e. liking
6. a **coveted** position   a. stolen   b. desired   c. feared   d. converted
   e. rejected
7. a(n) **implacable** enemy   a. calm   b. incomprehensible
   c. appeasable   d. smug   e. pacific
8. their **apathetic** response   a. eager   b. suspicious   c. pathetic
   d. uninterested   e. pitiful
9. their innate **cupidity**   a. amorousness   b. philandering
   c. philanthropy   d. curiosity   e. fraternizing
10. to **placate** a foe   a. imitate   b. agitate   c. pacify   d. understand
    e. escape

EXERCISE 6B   Circle the letter of the sentence in which the word in bold-faced type is used incorrectly.

1. a. Although she had seemed a confirmed **misogamist**, she
      unexpectedly married in her sixties.
   b. In spite of his own **misogamy**, Mr. Woodhouse consented to
      Emma's marriage to Mr. Knightley.
   c. **Misogamy** declined when divorce laws were relaxed.
   d. His **misogamy** includes all women, even his mother and sister.
2. a. Wise travelers to primitive areas carry water purification tablets to
      prevent **dysentery.**
   b. Soldiers in the trenches during World War I contracted
      dysentery as a result of poor sanitation.
   c. Trekking in Nepal, she suffered terrible **dysentery** from the local
      water.
   d. Explorers stationed at the remote **dysentery** were required to
      carry a week's rations at all times.

  3. a. Despite her six marriages and recent engagement, she still claims to be a **misogynist.**
    b. Prejudice against women can be interpreted as a result of **misogyny.**
    c. His jokes betrayed a subtle **misogyny** that made his audience uncomfortable.
    d. He was such a **misogynist** that he refused to let the doctor set his broken leg because she was a woman.

  4. a. Stirred by the **pathos** of the poor, Jane Addams established settlement houses that offered food, education, and support.
    b. The **pathos** roused by *Uncle Tom's Cabin,* which depicted the horrors of slavery, helped fuel the antislavery movement.
    c. When the show was cancelled and tickets were not refunded, the audience felt **pathos.**
    d. Napoleon addressed the victorious army in a speech of great **pathos,** urging them to eradicate the enemy.

  5. a. Only after many months did he discover that she was a **pathological** liar, unable to recognize her own falsehoods.
    b. Doctors found no **pathological** explanation for the patient's sudden paralysis.
    c. Police suspect a **pathological** criminal in the recent crimes.
    d. Mother Teresa won the Nobel Peace Prize for her great **pathology** toward the poor.

EXERCISE 6C

Fill in each blank with the most appropriate word from Lesson 6. Use a word or any of its forms only once.

1. He was diagnosed as ___Dyslexic___ when he still had difficulty reading in fifth grade.

2. Having suffered eight consecutive defeats, the members of the team felt understandably _____ before their last game of the season.

3. Newspaper stories about the homeless evoke feelings of ___Pathos___ in many readers.

4. He remained a life-long bachelor, a(n) ___misogamist___, although he had many close women friends.

5. I do not ___covet___ her position as director so much as the salary that goes with it.

6. Even during bombing raids, the nurse remained _____ and efficiently tended the wounded.

7. In *Wuthering Heights,* Heathcliff's _____ hatred could not be satisfied with revenge on only a single generation of the Linton family.

8. _____ drove the couple to acquire more cars, clothes, and appliances than they could ever use.

9. Since most children fear the dark, a child's insistence on having a night-light should not be considered _____.

REVIEW EXERCISES FOR LESSONS 5 AND 6

1 Circle the letter of the best answer to the following analogies and questions about roots and definitions.

1. Which Greek word means the same as Latin *amare?*
   a. *philein*   b. *pathos*   c. *misein*   d. *phobos*   e. *placare*
2. Which word is an antonym for *Francophobe?*
   a. Francophile   b. antipofranc   c. Francopath   d. Francodium
   e. misofranco
3. misanthrope : philanthrope : :
   a. bibliophobe : bibliophile
   b. *phobos* : fear
   c. apathy : empathy
   d. *dys* : pathos
   e. *amicus* : *amo*
4. inimical : amicable : :
   a. apathy : interest
   b. cupid : love
   c. pathological : diseased
   d. misogynist : woman
   e. odious : without scent
5. Which word is not derived from *pax, pacis,* "peace"?
   a. pacifier   b. pacifist   c. pacific   d. placid   e. appease

2 Substitute the appropriate word from Lessons 5 or 6 for each word or phrase in parentheses in the following paragraphs. No word is used more than once.

1. The discovery in 2000 of Captain William Kidd's ship Adventure, which sank in the Indian Ocean 300 years ago, has given historians and archeologists the kind of opportunity they

   _____covet_____ (crave). Kidd began his sailing career as a privateer, employed to protect British vessels in foreign waters; but he later became a pirate, and therefore was

   _____ (hostile) to government interests.

Owning property in New York and amassing considerable wealth

made him vulnerable to charges of _____ *covet* _____
(avarice), especially in the latter part of his career. When his

government investors required a scapegoat to ___ *placate* ___
(placate) factions in India, Kidd was hanged for piracy in 1701.

2. In middle age, Emily Dickinson developed an ___ *pathological* ___

    (abnormal) ___ *antipaty* ___ (dislike) for appearing in

    public. This quality, combined with her ___ *bibliophile* ___
    (love of books), led the poet, once known as the Belle of Amherst,

    to spend the last years of her life in ___ *pacific* ___
    (calm) and peaceful seclusion.

3 Writing or Discussion Activities

1. Describe real-life situations in which you have experienced (or
    observed someone else experiencing) each of the following feelings.
    Write one or two sentences for each situation. Use the following
    words in your answers.
    a. apathy *apatetic to empathy*
    b. empathy
    c. xenophobia *xenophobes*
    d. antipathy
    e. amity

2. Write a dialogue between a dissatisfied customer and the manager of
    some kind of business. Let their discussion reach some clear
    conclusion. Use at least five of these words (or some form of them)
    in your dialogue.

pacify	inimical	complacent
placate	odious	placid
appease	amity	amicable

LESSONS 7 AND 8

Creature Comforts

LESSON 7

Hic . . . mollesque sub arbore somni.
Here [are] soft slumbers under a tree.—VIRGIL

Key Words

ablution	domicile	somnambulate
deluge	domineer	somnolent
divest	dominion	travesty
domain	dormant	vested
domestic	investiture	vestment

Familiar Words
condominium
dome

Challenge Word
major-domo

DOMUS <L. "house"

1. **domicile** (dŏm′ ə sīl, dŏm′ ə səl, dōm′ ə sīl)
   n. A home; residence.

   A condominium complex may contain many separate **domiciles,** often of different sizes and designs.

2. **domestic** (də mĕs′ tĭk)
   adj. 1. Related to the family or household.

As our assigned **domestic** chore, my brother and I do the laundry.

2. Tame; trained to live with humans.

In India, elephants are **domestic** animals used for lifting heavy loads.

3. Indigenous to a particular country; native.

Domestic blue cheese resembles Italian gorgonzola and English stilton cheeses.

domestically, *adv.*; **domesticate**, *v.*

Familiar Words
dominate
domino
dungeon

Challenge Words
demesne
duenna

DOMINUS <L. "head of household," "lord," "master"

3. **domain**   (dō mān′)
   n. Range of one's control; territory.

The sandbox and sliding boards on our playground are the kindergartners' **domain.**

4. **domineer**   (dŏm′ ə nîr′)
   tr. and *intr. v.* To dominate; to be bossy.

David Copperfield's stepfather, Mr. Murdstone, **domineers** both David and his gentle mother.

domineering, *adj.*

5. **dominion**   (də mĭn′ yən)
   n. Control; rule; area of influence.

The Danes struggled to free their country from the **dominion** of Germany during World War II.

Familiar Words
dormitory

DORMIO, DORMIRE, DORMIVI, DORMITUM <L. "to sleep"

6. **dormant**   (dôr′ mənt)
   adj. Asleep; not in an active state.

Grandma Moses' artistic talent lay **dormant** until she began to paint at age seventy.

Familiar Words
insomnia

SOMNUS <L. "sleep"

7. **somnambulate**   (sŏm năm′ byə lāt)   [*ambulare* <L. "to walk around"]
   intr. v. To walk while sleeping.

Although many children **somnambulate,** most outgrow this involuntary activity by adulthood.

somnambulation, *n.*; **somnambulism**, *n.*; **somnambulist**, *n.*

8. **somnolent**   (sŏm′nə lənt)
adj. 1. Drowsy; sleepy.

We grew **somnolent** after our long hike in
the snow.

2. Causing sleep.

A warm bath before bedtime has a **somnolent**
effect.

LAVO, LAVARE, LAVI, LAUTUM <L. "to wash"

9. **ablution**   (ă blōō′ shən)   [*ab* <L. "away from"]
n. Washing of the body, especially as a ritual purification.

Most mosques have a central fountain where worshipers perform **ablutions** before entering to pray.

10. **deluge**   (dĕl′ yüj)   [*de* <L. "from," "away from"]
n. A downpour; a great flood.

When the dam broke, an entire village downstream was destroyed in
the **deluge.**

tr. v. To flood.

Reporters **deluged** Amelia Earhart with requests for interviews after her
historic transatlantic flight.

VESTIS <L. "garment"

11. **divest**   (dĭ vĕst′, dī vĕst′)   [*di* = *de* <L. "from," "away from"]
tr. v. 1. To take away something belonging to someone, especially a
right, title, or property; to dispossess.

After the Russian Revolution of 1917, members of the nobility were
divested of all titles and called "citizen" like everyone else.

2. To strip away, especially clothes.

Once Rosalind had **divested** herself of her disguise, the banished duke
immediately recognized her as his daughter.

divestment, *n.*; **divestiture,** *n.*

12. **investiture**   (ĭn vĕs′ tə choor′)   [*in* <L. "in"]
n. A ceremony in which a person formally receives the authority and
symbols of an office.

At her **investiture** as a Girl Scout, the Brownie received a pin and mem-
bership card.

investitive, *adj.*

13. **travesty** (trăv´ĭ stē) [*tra* = *trans* <L. "across" (indicating change)]
    n. An absurd or inferior imitation.

    The senior skit was a hilarious **travesty** of a faculty meeting.

    travesty, *v.*

14. **vestment** (vĕst´mənt)
    n. A garment that indicates position or
    authority, especially the robes worn by clergy.

    The simple woolen **vestment** and sandals of
    Franciscan friars reflect their vow of poverty.

15. **vested** (vĕs´tĭd)
    adj. 1. A concern for something from which a person expects to get
    personal benefit (used with *interest*).

    The judge disqualified herself because as the defendant's mother she
    had a **vested** interest in the case.

    2. Dressed, especially in vestments.

    An orchestra is traditionally **vested** in formal evening dress.

    3. Absolute; without question.

    All adult American citizens have the **vested** right to vote.

EXERCISE 7A

Circle the letter of the best SYNONYM (the word or phrase most nearly
the same as the word in bold-faced type).

1. such dangerous **somnambulation**   a. alcoholism   b. passivity
   c. sleep-walking   d. overeating   e. domestication
2. a **travesty** of justice   a. mockery   b. imitation   c. stripping away
   d. domicile   e. violation
3. perform **ablutions**   a. purifications   b. prayers   c. investitures
   d. festivals   e. rituals
4. a peculiar **domicile**   a. place to sleep   b. place to live
   c. dominion   d. refuge   e. authority

Circle the letter of the best ANTONYM (the word or phrase most nearly
opposite the word(s) in bold-faced type).

5. their **dormant** interest   a. destructive   b. somnolent   c. active
   d. undeveloped   e. domineering
6. **vested in** coronation robes   a. wearing   b. divested of   c. weighed
   down by   d. invested in   e. made uncomfortable by

7. a(n) **somnolent** lion   a. meat-eating   b. sleepy   c. alert
   d. domesticated   e. aged
8. of **domestic** manufacture   a. home-made   b. foreign   c. cosy
   d. peculiar   e. unknown

EXERCISE 7B   Circle the letter of the sentence in which the word in bold-faced type is used incorrectly.

1. a. We are **deluged** with orders in December.
   b. Our only bridge was swept away in the **deluge.**
   c. For forty days Noah's family waited for the **Deluge** to pass.
   d. Don't **deluge** yourself: there's never a weekend without homework.
2. a. She has a tendency to **domineer** in committee meetings.
   b. We need someone who can lead the class without **domineering.**
   c. May I **domineer** your bike this afternoon?
   d. Many adolescents rebel against a **domineering** parent.
3. a. Thoughtful campers take care not to let the soap from their **ablutions** get into streams or rivers.
   b. The **ablutions** would not remove the grass stains from her jeans.
   c. King Louis XIV's morning **ablutions** became a solemn court event.
   d. Before approaching the Delphic oracle to ask advice, Greek pilgrims first performed **ablutions** in the Castillian Spring.
4. a. Although my home is only a small apartment, it is my **domain.**
   b. I refuse to let you **domain** me any longer!
   c. Unfortunately these back problems are not my **domain**; let me recommend an orthopedic surgeon.
   d. Serfs were not allowed to leave the **domain** of their lord without permission.
5. a. Everyone has a **vested** interest in the community's quality of education.
   b. In the graduation procession faculty members are **vested** in academic gowns and hoods.
   c. "According to the authority **vested** in me by the state, I pronounce you husband and wife," said the Justice of the Peace.
   d. Speculators who **vested** their money in electronics made great fortunes.
6. a. Following land reform laws in the 1950s, wealthy landowners in China were subjected to forced **divestment** of their estates.
   b. To avoid conflicts of interest, cabinet members must **divest** themselves of all other positions.
   c. Pathological liars **divest** themselves of every shred of credibility.
   d. Try not to let the noise outside **divest** your attention from the examination.

EXERCISE 7C   Fill in each blank with the most appropriate word from Lesson 7. Use a word or any of its forms only once.

1. Bulbs planted during the fall remain _____ until spring.

2. The mitre, a tall, pointed hat, is part of a bishop's

    _____.

3. Greek temples such as the Parthenon were built as

    _____ for the deities.

4. At her _____ as chancellor of the university, she received the traditional staff of office.

5. Lady Macbeth, who walks through the castle washing her hands in

    her sleep, is perhaps the most famous _____ in literature.

6. That student is fortunate who is as comfortable in the

    _____ of math and science as in that of the humanities.

7. The armies of Alexander the Great established _____ over the entire Middle East.

LESSON 8

Mens sine pondere ludit.
The mind is playful when free from pressure.

Key Words		
allude	delusion	potable
carnivorous	elude	potion
collusion	herbivorous	precocious
concoct	imbibe	saline
cuisine	mellifluous	voracious

Familiar Words
apricot
biscuit
ricotta

COQUO, COQUERE, COXI, COCTUM
<L. "to cook"

1. **concoct** (kən kŏkt′)   [*con* = *cum* <L. "with"]
   tr. v. 1. To mix ingredients, as in cooking.

   We **concocted** a salad of exotic fruits.

   2. To invent or devise.

The friends tried to **concoct** a method for sending messages between their houses.

concoction, *n.*

2. **cuisine**   (kwĭ zēn′)
n. A characteristic style of cooking.

Mexican **cuisine** relies on corn, beans, chicken, beef, and chiles.

3. **precocious**   (prĭ kō′ shəs)   [*pre* = *prae* <L. "before"]
adj. Showing unusually early development, especially mentally.

Some **precocious** children can read at age three.

precocity, *n.*

Familiar Words
devour

VORO, VORARE, VORAVI, VORATUM <L. "to devour"

4. **carnivorous**   (kär nĭv′ ər əs)   [*caro, carnis* <L. "flesh"]
adj. Meat-eating.

Lions and other **carnivorous** animals have diets primarily of meat.

carnivore, *n.*

5. **herbivorous**   (hûr bĭv′ ər əs)   [*herba* <L. "plant"]
adj. Plant-eating.

Horses and cows are **herbivorous** animals.

herbivore, *n.*

NOTA BENE: *Vorare* provides the suffix -*vore*, "eater of," and -*vorous*, "eating," which are used to indicate what a creature eats. In this lesson you have *carnivorous* (*caro* <L. "flesh") and *herbivorous* (*herb* <L. "plant"). An *omnivore* (*omni* <L. "all"), such as a human being, eats all kinds of food. Other less frequent combinations include *granivorous* (*granum* <L. "grain"), "grain-eating"; *insectivorous*, "insect-eating"; and *piscivorous* (*pisci* <L. "fish"), "fish-eating."

6. **voracious**   (vô rā′ shəs, və rā′ shəs)
adj. 1. Extremely hungry; greedy.

The backpackers had **voracious** appetites after hiking all day.

2. Eager for some activity or interest.

A **voracious** reader of science fiction, she had read the library's entire collection.

voracity, *n.*

MEL, MELLIS <L. "honey"

7. **mellifluous**   (mə lĭf′ lōō əs)   [*fluere* <L. "to flow"]
   adj. Sweet as honey (referring to voice or words).

   The aria ended with a **mellifluous** blend of soprano and flute.

SAL <L. "salt"

8. **saline**   (sā′lēn, sā′līn)
   adj. Having to do with salt.

   Freshwater animals cannot survive in a **saline** environment.

BIBO, BIBERE, BIBI, BIBITUM
<L. "to drink"

9. **imbibe**   (ĭm bīb′)   [*im* = *in* <L. "in," "inside"]
   tr. v. 1. To drink.

   The Olympian gods of Greek mythology eat ambrosia and **imbibe** nectar.

   2. To absorb; to take in.

   The best way to **imbibe** woodworking technique is to watch an expert carpenter.

   imbiber, *n.*

POTO, POTARE, POTAVI, POTUM <L. "to drink"

10. **potable**   (pō′tə bəl)
    adj. Fit to drink.

    Because a chemical spill had contaminated local wells, the water was not **potable** for several weeks.

11. **potion**   (pō′ shən)
    n. A liquid for drinking, especially a medicinal, magic, or poisonous drink.

    Once Tristan and Isolde drank the magic **potion**, they fell deeply in love.

LUDO, LUDERE, LUSI, LUSUM <L. "to play"

12. **allude**   (ə lōōd′)   [*al* = *ad* <L. "to," "toward"]
    intr. v. To make an indirect reference to.

Challenge Words
illusive
illusory
interlude
ludicrous
postlude

We sometimes **allude** to Shakespeare as the Bard of Stratford-upon-Avon.

allusion, *n.*; **allusive**, *adj.*

13. **collusion** (kə loo′ zhən) [*col* = *cum* <L. "with," "together"]
   n. A secret agreement for a deceitful purpose; conspiracy.

   Auditors discovered **collusion** by the managers in an attempt to defraud the company.

   collude, *v.*; **collusive**, *adj.*

14. **delusion** (dĭ loo′ zhən, dĭ lyoo′ zhən) [*de* <L. "from," "away from"]
   n. 1. A false belief or opinion, especially one held in spite of contradictory evidence.

   Even after she played three years in the WNBA, her parents maintained their **delusion** that she would be a surgeon.

   2. A deception.

   The pigs in George Orwell's *Animal Farm* foster the **delusion** that they deserve special privileges forbidden other animals.

   delude, *v.*; **deluded**, *adj.*; **delusioned**, *adj.*

15. **elude** (ĭ lood′) [*e* = *ex* <L. "from," "out of"]
   tr. v. 1. To avoid or escape from by cunning; to evade.

   The bandits **eluded** their pursuers.

   2. To escape detection; to baffle.

   The solution to that math problem **eludes** me.

   elusion, *n.*; **elusive**, *adj.*

   NOTA BENE: Don't confuse *delude* and *elude*. If something *deludes* you, it tricks or misleads you. False advertising, for example, may delude you by misrepresenting a product. If something *eludes* you, you can't grasp it, either literally (The escaped canary eluded capture) or figuratively (The solution to this equation eluded the class).

EXERCISE 8A

Circle the letter of the best SYNONYM (the word or phrase most nearly the same as the word in bold-faced type).

1. to **concoct** a plan   a. spoil   b. put together   c. discover
   d. explain   e. improve
2. an unsuspected **collusion**   a. collision   b. combination
   c. cooperation   d. difficulty   e. conspiracy

3. a(n) **mellifluous** name   a. smoothly flowing   b. affectionate
   c. famous   d. short   e. long
4. a fabulous **potion**   a. drink   b. inheritance   c. jewel   d. share of
   something   e. ruler
5. appreciate French **cuisine**   a. wine   b. cooking methods   c. taste
   d. fashion design   e. kitchens

Circle the letter of the best ANTONYM (the word or phrase most nearly opposite the word in bold-faced type).

6. make the medicine more **potable**   a. elusive   b. transportable
   c. effective   d. undrinkable   e. stable
7. a cruel **delusion**   a. plot   b. truth   c. evasion   d. suggestion
   e. deception
8. the **voracious** theatergoer   a. eager   b. critical   c. domineering
   d. somnolent   e. indifferent

EXERCISE 8B   Circle the letter of the sentence in which the word in bold-faced type is used incorrectly.

1. a. Give him some vegetables, herbs, and cream, and he'll **concoct** a
      tasty soup.
   b. You **concoct** me every time I start to say something.
   c. We're **concocting** a surprise party for the twins.
   d. This tofu **concoction** tastes like ice cream but contains no milk.
2. a. The meaning of their winks and nudges **eluded** me completely.
   b. Hiding in the "Secret Annex," Anne Frank's family **eluded** the
      Nazis for two years.
   c. The Scarlet Pimpernel, Baroness Orczy's crafty hero, proved so
      elusive that he was never detected by French officials.
   d. She waited for her parents to make some **elusion** to the dented
      fender.
3. a. Despite his distaste for **collusion**, Brutus joined Cassius's plot
      against Caesar.
   b. Stalin's fear of **collusion** within the Communist party led him to
      arrest even long-time party members during the 1930s.
   c. By this delicate surgery a patient's heart **collusion** can be
      repaired.
   d. Working in **collusion** with the Allies during World War II, the
      French Resistance prepared for the invasion of Normandy.

4. a. He **imbibed** a strong sense of Southern tradition from his grandmother.

    b. No soda, thank you; I never **imbibe** sugary drinks.

    c. She felt great urgency to **imbibe** as much of Rome as possible during her brief visit.

    d. I **imbibed** a few cookies to keep from starving before lunch.

5. a. **Saline** lake water is not potable.

    b. Cucumbers preserved in a **saline** solution become pickles.

    c. Although her **saline** interruptions irritated the speaker, they raised interesting points.

    d. Objects float more easily in **saline** waters.

6. a. Despite her mathematical **precocity**, she is socially immature.

    b. Anthropologists have noted a trend toward **precocious** adolescence among South Sea islanders.

    c. Tutored by his father, English philosopher John Stuart Mill had the **precocious** ability to translate Greek at the age of four.

    d. Because the soufflé was still **precocious** when removed from the oven, it fell into a soggy mass.

7. a. After my low test scores, I have no **delusions** about becoming valedictorian.

    b. Only **delusions** of grandeur could lead a beginner like her to challenge a grand master in chess.

    c. Extreme desert heat can create an optical **delusion** known as a Fata Morgana.

    d. You are **deluded** if you think I'm going to lend you my new sweater.

EXERCISE 8C   Fill in each blank with the most appropriate word from Lesson 8. Use a word or any of its forms only once.

1. Fierce teeth and claws identify Tyrannosaurus Rex as a(n)

    _____ who preyed on other animals.

2. Although everyone else greatly enjoyed it, I did not think the

    Tibetan tea made with salt and yak butter was _____.

3. The crowd listened rapturously to soprano Leontyne Price's

    _____ voice.

4. After two months at sea, the sailors were _____ for fresh fruits and vegetables.

5. Giraffes are _____, feeding on mimosa and acacia trees.

6. Friar Lawrence gave Juliet a(n) _____ that would make her fall into a death-like sleep for several days after she drank it.

7. Dutch _____, which has been influenced by the Netherlands' Asian colonies, includes many curry and rice dishes.

8. That lecture was so disorganized that the point of it simply _____ me.

9. The proud parents took every opportunity to _____ to their daughter's successful career.

REVIEW EXERCISES FOR LESSONS 7 AND 8

1 Circle the letter of the best answer to the following analogies and questions about roots and definitions.

1. *dormire* : *lavare* : :
   a. sleep : eat
   b. dormitory : lavatory
   c. *bibere* : *potare*
   d. *mel* : honey
   e. eat : sleep

2. *potare* : water : :
   a. *domire* : sleep
   b. *vorare* : bread
   c. *coquere* : pan
   d. *ludere* : delude
   e. *lavare* : water

3. Which word is not derived from *ludere*?
   a. collusion   b. illusion   c. prelude   d. ablution   e. allude

4. Which root is not related to drinking or eating?
   a. *coquere*   b. *vorare*   c. *ludere*   d. *potare*   e. *bibere*

5. Which root is defined incorrectly?
   a. *somnus*   <L.   "sleep"
   b. *ludere*   <L.   "to play"
   c. *bibere*   <L.   "to drink"
   d. *domus*   <L.   "dome"
   e. *vestis*   <L.   "garment"

2 Substitute the appropriate word from Lessons 7 or 8 for each word or phrase in parentheses in the following paragraphs. No word is used more than once.

1. Although a semiliterate peasant, Rasputin came to _____ (dominate) the _____ (household life) of the Russian imperial family. The Tsarina Alexandra held to the

   _____ (false belief) that Rasputin could heal her only son and heir to the Russian throne, who suffered from incurable hemophilia. Appalled by Rasputin's misuse of power,

   courtiers finally _____ (conspired) to have him assassinated.

2. In the _____ (field) of televised cooking experts, several men and women have become nationally acclaimed

   for their creative _____ (inventions).

   _____ (Greedy) viewers never miss programs offering novel ideas for the kitchen. Cultural historians credit these TV cooking shows with having radically altered the American

   _____ (style of food preparation).

3 Writing or Discussion Activities

1. Children are often described as precocious in some way. Write a paragraph describing someone who is or was precocious, perhaps someone you know. Include in your paragraph specific examples of behavior to illustrate this child's "unusually early development."

2. Write a sentence for each of the following words or phrases, describing a situation in which you or someone else could be described as
   a. being in collusion.
   b. deluded.
   c. having a vested interested in something.
   d. having a dormant talent.
   e. domineering.

3. In this passage from *Macbeth,* Shakespeare describes three witches concocting a magic potion:

First Witch: Round about the cauldron go;
    In the poisoned entrails throw.
    Toad, that under cold stone
    Days and nights has thirty-one
    Sweltered venom sleeping got,
    Boil thou first in the charmed pot.

All: Double, double toil and trouble;
    Fire burn, and cauldron bubble.

Second Witch: Fillet of a fenny snake,
    In the cauldron boil and bake;
    Eye of newt, and toe of frog,
    Wool of bat, and tongue of dog,
    Adder's fork, and blind-worm's sting,
    Lizard's leg, and howlet's wing—
    For a charm of powerful trouble,
    Like a hell-broth boil and bubble.

All: Double, double toil and trouble;
    Fire burn, and cauldron bubble.

Third Witch: Scale of dragon, tooth of wolf,
    Witches' mummy, maw and gulf
    Of the ravin'd salt-sea shark,
    Root of hemlock digged i' the dark. . . .

All: Double, double toil and trouble;
    Fire burn, and cauldron bubble.

Invent your own concoction using ingredients available in the contemporary world.
a. First list the ingredients that would go into your concoction.
b. Then describe how to prepare the brew.
c. Finally, explain what effect the potion is supposed to have.

PART TWO

From Head to Toe

The Head

Directions

1. Determine how the Latin or Greek root is related in meaning and spelling to each defined—KEY—word that follows it.
2. Learn the pronunciation and definition(s) of each KEY word, and notice how the words are used in sentences.
3. Practice using the varied forms of KEY words.
4. Build your knowledge with all the information given: Latin mottoes, Familiar Words, Challenge Words, and Nota Bene references.
5. Complete the exercises.

LESSON 9

Frons est animi janua.
The face is the door of the soul.—QUINTUS CICERO

Key Words		
affront	confront	facade
capitalist	decapitate	facet
capitulation	deface	precipice
cerebral	efface	precipitate
cerebration	effrontery	recapitulation

Familiar Words
cap
capital
capital letter
capitalize
capitol
captain
chapter
chief
kerchief
mischief
recap

Challenge Words
cap-a-pie
capitation
per capita

CAPUT, CAPITIS <L. "head"

1. **capitalist**   (kăp′ə təl ĭst)
   n. 1. A person who has invested personal wealth in business.

   Having completed his first automobile in 1892, Henry Ford went on to become a **capitalist** in the Ford Motor Company.

   2. A very wealthy person.

   Some **capitalists,** such as Gloria Swanson, became wealthy by acting in silent films.

   capitalism, *n.;* **capitalistic,** *adj.;* **capitalize,** *v.*

2. **capitulation**   (kə pĭch′ o͞o lā′shən)
   n. Surrender; ending resistance.

   Famine forced the besieged city's **capitulation.**

   capitulate, *v.*

3. **decapitate**   (dĭ kăp′ə tāt)   [*de* <L. "from," "away from"]
   tr. v. To cut off the head of; to behead.

   In 1793 the French revolutionaries **decapitated** Louis XVI.

4. **precipice**   (prĕs′ə pĭs)   [*pre* = *prae* <L. "before"]
   n. A very steep or vertical face of a cliff or rock.

   Inexperienced climbers should not try to scale the **precipice.**

   2. The edge of a dangerous situation.

   The nation stood on the **precipice** of war.

5. **precipitate**   (prĭ sĭp′ə tāt)   [*pre* = *prae* <L. "before"]
   tr. v. 1. To throw down from a great height.

   The earthquake **precipitated** boulders into the canyon.

   2. To make happen suddenly or quickly.

   In 1955 Rosa Parks **precipitated** civil rights demonstrations by asserting the right of blacks to sit in front seats of buses.

   NOTA BENE: The verb *precipitate* can also mean to cause condensation in the form of rain or snow, i.e., *precipitation.*

adj. (prĭ sĭp′ə tət′) Speeding along heedlessly; headstrong.

Juliet is **precipitate** in deciding to marry Romeo after knowing him only a few hours.

precipitant, *adj.* and *n.*; **precipitation**, *n.*; **precipitous**, *adj.*

6. **recapitulation** (rē kə pĭch′ ōō lā′shən) [*re* <L. "back," "again"]
n. 1. The restatement of a main idea.

The instructor's **recapitulation** during the lecture helped the students understand the complex mathematical theory.

2. A summary or concise review.

Your **recapitulation** of the movie's plot convinces me I ought to see it.

recap, *n.* and *v.*; **recapitulate**, *v.*

CEREBRUM <L. "brain"

Challenge Words
cerebellum
cerebral cortex
cerebral palsy

7. **cerebral** (sĕr ē′brəl)

adj. 1. Pertaining to the brain.

The **cerebral** tumor required opening the skull for delicate surgery.

2. Intellectual.

She prefers **cerebral** conversations to aimless chatter.

cerebrum, *n.*

8. **cerebration** (sĕr ə brā′shən)
n. The action of thinking; thought.

Philosopher Hannah Arendt provoked scholarly **cerebration** and controversy on such subjects as justice, morality, and the nature of evil.

cerebrate, *v.*

FACIES <L. "face," "form," "shape"

Familiar Words
face
face-off
face-saving
facial
surface
typeface

9. **deface** (dĭ fās′) [*de* <L. "from," "away from"]
tr. v. To mar or spoil the appearance or surface of (something).

Air pollution from tourist buses has begun to **deface** the monoliths of Stonehenge in southern England.

defacement, *n.*

10. efface (ĭ fās′)   [*e = ex* <L. "from," "out of"]
     tr. v. 1. To wipe out; to obliterate. Also, to make less clear, as if rubbing out.

Time has not **effaced** the horror of the Holocaust.

2. To make oneself inconspicuous.

Celebrities sometimes try to **efface** themselves in a crowd when they tire of constant attention.

11. facade (fə säd′)
     n. 1. A face of a building.

The Capitol in Washington, D.C., has a neoclassical **facade.**

2. The face or front of anything, especially an artificial or false front.

Her **facade** of poverty concealed a life of fortune.

12. facet (făs′ it)
     n. 1. One of the many sides of a cut stone or jewel.

Gems with a "brilliant" cut have fifty-eight **facets.**

2. One aspect of a situation, or of a tooth.

In her autobiography Maya Angelou reveals the many **facets** of her personality and experience.

FRONS, FRONTIS <L. "front," "forehead," "face"

13. affront (ə frŭnt′)   [*af = ad* <L. "to," "toward"]
     tr. v. To insult intentionally; to offend or embarrass.

A guest's ostentatiously bad table manners may **affront** the hosts and other guests.

n. An insult or offensive act.

People sometimes mistake constructive criticism for a personal **affront.**

14. confront (kən frŭnt′)   [*con = cum* <L. "with"]
     tr. v. 1. To stand or come directly in front of.

It is usually more productive to **confront** obstacles than to pretend they don't exist.

2. To face with defiance or hostility.

The Confederate forces **confronted** the Northern troops with a barrage of artillery fire.

confrontation, *n.*

15. **effrontery** (ĭ frŭn′ tə rē)   [*e* = *ex* <L. "from," "out of"]

    n. Flippant or insulting boldness; audacity.

    They had the **effrontery** to push ahead of me in line and then to buy the last tickets.

EXERCISE 9A

Circle the letter of the best SYNONYM (the word or phrase most nearly the same as the word in bold-faced type).

1. Napoleon's **capitulation** at Waterloo   a. resentment   b. surrender
   c. leadership   d. headgear   e. confusion
2. to **efface** a clue   a. discover   b. affront   c. provide   d. ignore
   e. erase
3. concentrated **cerebration**   a. searching   b. effort   c. thought
   d. enjoyment   e. memorization
4. to **decapitate** the offender   a. dehumanize   b. behead
   c. undercut   d. capture   e. remove the hat of
5. the **effrontery** of careless people   a. discourtesy   b. adoration
   c. honesty   d. silliness   e. display

Circle the letter of the best ANTONYM (the word or phrase most nearly opposite the word in bold-faced type).

6. a spectacular **facade**   a. front   b. back   c. shape   d. profile
   e. face
7. an unexpected **affront**   a. act of kindness   b. scolding
   c. challenge   d. insult   e. escape
8. to **deface** the statue   a. carve   b. mask   c. disfigure   d. name
   e. repair
9. to **confront** the attackers   a. taunt   b. retreat from   c. confuse
   d. face   e. criticize
10. a **precipitate** remark   a. hasty   b. rash   c. thoughtful
    d. anticipated   e. self-effacing

EXERCISE 9B

Circle the letter of the sentence in which the word in bold-faced type is used incorrectly.

1. a. The jeweler carefully cut each **facet** of the sapphire.
   b. The young athlete claimed to be especially good at the **facet** of discus-throwing.

    c. A biographer must explore every **facet** of the subject's life.

    d. The **facets** of a grasshopper's eye are visible only under a microscope.

2. a. Several guests who received a last-minute **recapitulation** to the party decided not to attend.

    b. We expect a lecture to conclude when the speaker begins to **recapitulate** the main points.

    c. A study of history reveals that events are often a **recapitulation** of the past.

    d. **Recapitulation** of melody is an important element in music.

3. a. Behind a **facade** of confidence the young gymnast quivered with anxiety.

    b. The salesclerk recommended a washable **facade** to protect my clothing.

    c. Visitors to Hollywood film studios are often surprised to see mansions and main streets that have only **facades.**

    d. The **facades** of Gothic cathedrals are often decorated with statues of saints and biblical figures.

4. a. Choosing a college should not be a **precipitate** decision.

    b. The assassination of Austrian Archduke Franz Ferdinand and Archduchess Sophie in Sarajevo, Yugoslavia, **precipitated** World War I.

    c. When mountain snow begins to melt, experts often save lives by **precipitating** avalanches.

    d. Fortune-sellers allow people to **precipitate** the future.

5. a. The physicists who discovered the principle of the black hole have spent thousands of hours in **cerebral** activity.

    b. The basketball star enjoys both sports and **cerebral** games.

    c. The graduates wore robes of **cerebral** blue.

    d. The **cerebral** cortex is composed chiefly of gray matter responsible for important nervous responses in the body.

6. a. After only two weeks on the job, the shipping clerk had the **effrontery** to ask for a raise.

    b. The marathon runner's trademark was her orange **effrontery.**

    c. A reporter had the **effrontery** to ask the hostess if her diamonds were real.

    d. Until this century, a well-born bridegroom in China would be guilty of **effrontery** if he tried to meet his bride before the wedding.

7. a. After knocking over a china vase, the dog scampered off to **efface** itself in a far corner of the room.

    b. Decades of harsh weather had **effaced** the names on the tombstones.

    c. Leonardo da Vinci sometimes **effaced** drawings by painting over them.

    d. The preservation society **effaced** the historic house with paint of the original color.

8. a. In the last battle, Macduff keeps his sword unbloodied until he can **confront** the tyrant Macbeth and decapitate him.
b. **Confronted** by six pairs of prancing gray horses, the royal carriage moved briskly past the cheering crowds.
c. In pressing for women's voting rights, Elizabeth Cady Stanton precipitated **confrontation** with opponents and police.
d. Even veteran actors like the late Laurence Olivier sometimes experience stagefright when they **confront** an audience.
9. a. Time and weather had **defaced** the bronze Venetian horses.
b. Early restorers of the Sistine Chapel in Rome unintentionally **defaced** some of Michelangelo's painted figures.
c. The actors used an efficacious cold cream to **deface** themselves after a performance.
d. Strip mining has been outlawed in some places because the process causes severe **defacement** of land.

EXERCISE 9C   Fill in each blank with the most appropriate word from Lesson 9. Use a word or any of its forms only once.

1. Even skilled mountaineers may feel some fear when they look up at a(n) _____precipice_____ they are about to climb.
2. The _____facade_____ of the White House is a popular subject for photographers.
3. To _____decapitate_____ political offenders by guillotine as a public spectacle gave power to the revolutionists.
4. Scholars can thank the computer for saving them many hours of _____cerebration_____ and computation.
5. The _____capitalist_____ attributed his wealth to thrifty progenitors, wise investments, and good luck.
6. The army sergeant declared that any lapse of discipline among the new recruits would be a personal _____affront_____.

LESSON 10

Orator fit, poeta nascitur.
An orator is made; a poet is born.

Key Words

disgorge	indenture	orthodontist
gargantuan	inexorable	osculate
gargoyle	oracle	regurgitate
gorge	oration	supercilious
indentation	orifice	trident

SUPERCILIUM <L. "eyebrow"

1. **supercilious** (sōō′ pər sĭl′ ē əs) [*super* <L. "above" + *cilium* <L. "eyelid." (A lifted eyebrow conveys an impression of haughtiness.)] *adj.* Disdainful; haughty and aloof.

   The casually dressed newcomers received **supercilious** looks from the other guests at the formal party.

   superciliously, *adv.*; **superciliousness,** *n.*

OS, ORIS <L. "mouth"
ORO, ORARE, ORAVI, ORATUM <L. "to speak"

Familiar Words
adore
oral

2. **inexorable** (ĭn ĕk′ sər ə bəl) [*in* <L. "not"; *ex* <L. "out," "forth"] *adj.* Relentless; unyielding.

   Arctic explorers respect the **inexorable** force of winter storms.

Challenge Words
oratorio
orotund
peroration

3. **oracle** (ôr′ə kəl, ŏ′rə kəl)
   n. 1. A shrine where the ancient Greeks consulted one of their gods for advice or prophecy.

   The **oracle** at Eleusis was sacred to the goddess Demeter.

   2. A prophecy made at such a shrine.

   An **oracle** sometimes came in the form of a thunder clap or a flight of birds.

   3. A person who transmits prophecy from a deity.

   The **oracle** of Apollo at Delphi was a succession of young women known as Pythia.

4. A person or thing regarded as able to give wise guidance.

She is considered a stock market **oracle.**

oracular, *adj.*

4. **oration** (ô rā′shən)
n. An address or formal speech given on a special occasion.

In 1963 Martin Luther King, Jr. stirred civil rights supporters with his "I Have a Dream" **oration** at the Lincoln Memorial.

orate, *v.*; **orator,** *n.*; **oratorical,** *adj.*; **oratory,** *n.*

5. **orifice** (ôr′ə fĭs, ôr′ĭ fĭs) [-*fice* <L. *ficere* or *facere*, "to make"]
n. A mouth or vent; an opening.

Flames erupted from the **orifice** of the great volcano.

6. **osculate** (ŏs′kyə lāt) [*osculum* <L. "kiss"]
tr. and *intr. v.* To kiss (usually used playfully).

The newlyweds **osculated** under the mistletoe.

osculation, *n.*

DENS, DENTIS <L. "tooth"

7. **indentation** (ĭn′ dĕn tā′shən) [*in* <L. "in"]
n. A cut or notch.

Fjords are narrow waterways formed by deep **indentations** of land along the Norwegian coast.

8. **indenture** (ĭn dĕn′chər) [*in* <L. "in." (*Indenture* takes its meaning from the practice of cutting a document in half with identifying notches or by making identical notches in copies of a contract.)]
n. 1. A written contract between two parties.

The **indenture** established each partner's responsibilities.

2. (usually plural) An agreement binding an apprentice to work for a master.

The **indentures** stated the length of the workers' apprenticeship.

tr. v. To bind by written contract.

Many early immigrants **indentured** themselves to pay for their passage to America.

Familiar Words
dandelion
dental
dentifrice
dentist
dentistry
denture
indent

Challenge Words
dentin
dentition
indention

9. **trident**   (trīd′ənt)   [*tri = tres* <L. "three"]
   n. A long three-pronged fork or weapon.

   The Roman god Neptune, known to the Greeks as Poseidon, is often pictured with his **trident.**

ODON, ODONTOS <G. "tooth"

10. **orthodontist**   (ôr′ thə dŏn′tist)   [*ortho* <G. "straight," "correct"]
    n. A specialist who corrects irregularly positioned teeth.

    The **orthodontist** expertly fitted braces on my teeth.

    orthodontia, *n.*; **orthodontics,** *n.*

GURGES, GURGITIS <L. "throat," "whirlpool"

11. **gorge**   (gôrj)
    n. 1. A deep, narrow passage with rocky sides, enclosed between mountains.

    Negotiating both **gorges** and precipices, Gertrude Benham became the first woman to climb Mount Kilimanjaro.

    2. Gluttonous eating.

    Many people go on diets after a **gorge** during the holidays.

    3. A feeling of nausea (used with *rise*).

    The smell of decay made my **gorge** rise.

    intr. v. 1. To eat greedily.

    After a day of strenuous climbing in the Himalayas, the team **gorged** on chocolate.

    2. To fill full; to stuff.

    European museums are **gorged** with tourists, especially in the summer.

12. **disgorge**   (dĭs gôrj′)   [*dis* <L. "away from," "apart"]
    tr. v. 1. To expel from the throat or stomach; to vomit.

    The baby disgorged the marble it had swallowed.

    2. To discharge violently.

    Rocks and lava **disgorged** by the Hawaiian volcano Mauna Loa have increased the size of the mountain.

13. **gargantuan** (gär găn′chŏŏ ən)

    adj. Of immense size; gigantic. (This word is based on the name of the legendary giant Gargantua, whose name Francois Rabelais used in his satire *Gargantua* about a character who had enormous intellectual and physical appetites. Although this word is not directly linked with classical Latin, its literary association and surmised derivation from *gurges* warrant it a place here.)

    According to legend, the giant lumberjack Paul Bunyan created the Great Lakes so his **gargantuan** blue ox would have sufficient drinking water.

14. **gargoyle** (gär′goil′)

    n. A grotesque carved human or animal figure, especially one used as a rainspout carrying water clear of a wall.

    Look up high for **gargoyles** on the Cathedral of Notre-Dame in Paris.

15. **regurgitate** (rē gûr′jə tāt′) [*re* <L. "back," "again"]

    tr. v. 1. To cause to pour back or cast up partially digested food; to vomit.

    Some birds **regurgitate** semi-digested food to feed their young.

    2. To rush or surge back.

    We watched the sea caves **regurgitate** the tide.

EXERCISE 10A

Circle the letter of the best SYNONYM (the word or phrase most nearly the same as the word in bold-faced type).

1. to **osculate**   a. waver   b. slap   c. kiss   d. float   e. whisper
2. a substantial **indenture**   a. set of false teeth   b. bite   c. apprentice   d. contract   e. cut in pay
3. a powerful **oration**   a. debate   b. shout   c. speech   d. explanation   e. monologue

Circle the letter of the best ANTONYM (the word or phrase most nearly opposite the word in bold-faced type).

4. a(n) **gargantuan** appetite   a. literary   b. dainty   c. moderate   d. carnivorous   e. enormous

5. to **disgorge** a piece of bone   a. break   b. spit out   (c.) digest
   d. gnaw   e. scrape
6. a **supercilious** manner   a. disdainful   b. questioning   c. comic
   (d.) humble   e. detached
7. a(n) **inexorable** decree   (a.) flexible   b. unyielding   c. unwise
   d. oracular   e. outspoken
8. to **gorge** at a banquet   a. cough   b. feel sick   c. chatter   (d.) eat
   lightly   e. mingle

EXERCISE 10B   Circle the letter of the sentence in which the word in bold-faced type is
used incorrectly.

1. a. The doctor forced the picnickers to **regurgitate** the poisonous
      mushrooms they had eaten.
   b. Make an argument; don't just **regurgitate** the facts.
   (c.) She returned to the airline office to have her ticket **regurgitated.**
   d. Baby condors feed on material that the parent bird **regurgitates.**
2. a. Followers of the goddess Artemis sought her **oracle** in her temple
      at Ephesus.
   b. Cassandra's **oracular** warning about Greek treachery was ignored
      by the Trojans, who were consequently defeated.
   c. In ancient Greece the **oracle** supplied divine inspiration that was,
      however, often mysterious.
   (d.) The new cereal featured **oracle**-sized granules of wheat.
3. a. Because the merger of the two corporations was so complicated,
      the **indenture** was many pages long.
   b. After serving as an apprentice, the young carpenter reclaimed his
      indentures and set up his own shop.
   c. The **indenture** restored land to Native Americans to whom it had
      once belonged.
   (d.) **Indentures** need to be carefully fitted by a dentist to make
      chewing easier.
4. (a.) After their angry confrontation, the debaters felt an icy **gorge** of
      hatred rise between them.
   b. The hungry patrons anticipated **gorging** themselves at the all-you-
      can-eat restaurant.
   c. Reading about the indiscriminate slaughter of gray whales made
      my **gorge** rise.
   d. Fossils excavated from Olduvai **Gorge** offer evidence that our
      ancestors had their beginnings in Africa.
5. a. Visitors wait eagerly for hours to see the geyser Old Faithful spout
      a fountain of water from its **orifice.**
   b. Describing the fertilization of orchids, Charles Darwin writes that
      "the **orifice** into the nectar-receptacle lies . . . close to the lower
      side of the flower."

c. After many hours workers rescued the child who had fallen through the **orifice** of the abandoned well.

d. The human head has eight **orifices.**

6. a. Some dictionaries have thumb-shaped **indentations** to mark alphabetical divisions.

b. An **indentation** of five spaces is the conventional way to indicate the start of a paragraph.

c. Failure to be invited to a special party can cause severe **indentation** of one's ego.

d. In carving the owl, the artisan made delicate **indentations** to simulate feathers.

EXERCISE 10C   Fill in each blank with the most appropriate word from Lesson 10. Use a word or any of its forms only once.

1. Eva Perón's charismatic personality was surely a factor in her _____inexorable_____ rise to power in Argentina.

2. The _____oration_____ of Cicero, a Roman author and consul, are still used as models for modern-day public speakers.

3. Rainwater splashed steadily from the mouth of the _____orifice_____ leering from the medieval tower.

4. Statues ranging in size from miniature to _____Gargantuan_____ attracted a large crowd at the arts festival.

5. Pioneers on their way West could sometimes follow trails made by the _____indention_____ of wagon wheels.

6. The scuba diver used a(n) _____trident_____ for protection against aggressive sharks.

7. Trains _____disgorge_____ thousands of soccer fans at the stadium in Rio de Janeiro.

8. In earlier times there were no _____indentures_____ to help people with crooked teeth and faulty bites.

9. Two million years of erosion by the Colorado River formed the _____gorge_____ we call the Grand Canyon.

10. Some people have considered Nostradamus a(n) _____oracle_____ for his predictions in the sixteenth century of events that have seemed to come true.

11. Many of the characters Alice meets in Wonderland behave in a(n) _____supercilious_____ manner—they are scornful of her confusion and regard her as ignorant.

REVIEW EXERCISES FOR LESSONS 9 AND 10

1 Circle the letter of the best answer to the following analogies and questions about roots and definitions.

1. capitulation : head : :
   a. regurgitation : mouth
   b. osculation : eye
   c. cerebration : brain
   d. precipitation : eyebrow
   e. supercilious : forehead
2. *facies* : facade : :
   a. *frons* : forehead
   b. *caput* : head
   c. *gurges* : throat
   d. *os* : orifice
   e. *cerebrum* : mind
3. Which Latin word means the same as *odon*?
   a. *gurges*
   b. *dens*
   c. *cerebrum*
   d. *frons*
   e. *caput*
4. Which pair does not contain words with a common root?
   a. orthodontist — oracle
   b. gargoyle — gorge
   c. capitalist — precipice
   d. facet — efface
   e. inexorable — oration
5. Which word is defined incorrectly?
   a. indenture — "contract"
   b. inexorable — "relentless"
   c. precipitate — "headstrong"
   d. effrontery — "front"
   e. osculate — "kiss"

2 Substitute the appropriate word from Lessons 9 or 10 for each word or phrase in parentheses in the following paragraphs. No word is used more than once.

1. Kilauea in Hawaii has the record as the longest-active volcano in the world. In addition to eruptions in its central core, numerous eruptions from ___orifices___ (openings) along rift

zones have ___*disporged*___ (violently discharged)
boiling lava, creating lava lakes. In 1790 a ___*gargantuan*___
(gigantic) explosion of steaming lava overwhelmed a section of the
Hawaiian army marching near the crater. A major eruption is
___*memorably*___ (relentlessly) followed by lava flow,
violent earthquakes, or tidal waves.

2. The hippopotamus is responsible for more human deaths than any
other African mammal. Although relatively harmless in its river

home, a hippo ___*gorging*___ (greedily eating) on
the river bank can become lethal to anyone who ___*affront*___
(offends) it. Fear ___*precipitates*___ (quickly) results in
the hippo's headlong gallop back to the nearest river, smashing
whoever or whatever is in the way. If you must ___*confront*___
(stand directly in front of) a hippopotamus, never get between it
and the water!

3 Writing or Discussion Activities

1. You are a newspaper reporter writing a story for the local paper.
Explain in a short paragraph the situation suggested by each of the
headlines below. Give details that would make interesting reading,
but make your account objective (impersonal) rather than subjective
(personal).
   a. Orthodontist Recapitulates the Causes of Inexorable Defacement
   of Dental Facets
   b. Gastronome Gorges on Gargantuan Feast
   c. Precipitate Osculation Affronts Supercilious Recipient

2. Each of the following sentences applies to a general situation.
   a. That was a precipitate move.
   b. She is a cerebral person.
   c. He is amazingly oracular.
   d. It was gargantuan.
   e. We confronted one another.
   f. What effrontery!

   Choose two of the sentences and for each of them write a short
   paragraph creating a complete picture through your specific details.
   Answer the following questions: where? who? what? when? and
   how?

The Body

LESSON 11

Mens sana in corpore sano.
A sound mind in a sound body.

Key Words		
accolade	concordance	corpulent
accord	cordial	corpus
carnage	corporal	décolletage
carrion	corporeal	incarnate
	corps	ossify

Familiar Words
carnation
carnival
carnivorous

Challenge Words
incarnadine

CARO, CARNIS <L. "flesh"

1. **carnage**   (kär′nĭj)
   n. The killing of many people; massacre (sometimes used metaphorically).

   Civil War photographs reveal the **carnage** that took place on many battlefields in both North and South.

2. **carrion**   (kăr′ē ən)
   n. Dead and decaying flesh.

   Vultures feed on **carrion.**

   adj. Pertaining to dead flesh.

   The beached whale gave off a foul, **carrion** odor.

3. **incarnate**   (ĭn kär′nĭt)   [*in* <L. "in"]
   adj. Embodied in human form.

   Mildred (Babe) Didrikson Zaharias, who won more tournaments and medals in more sports than anyone in the twentieth century, is athleticism **incarnate.**

   incarnation, *n.*

COLLUM <L. "neck"

> **Familiar Word**
> collar

4. **accolade**   (ăk′ə lād, ăk ə lād′)   [*ac* = *ad* <L. "to," "toward"]
   n. 1. Any honor, award, or expression of approval.

   Her opera received critical **accolades.**

   2. A ceremonial tap on the shoulder (dub) with the flat side of a sword.

   Sir Walter Raleigh knelt on the deck of his ship to receive Queen Elizabeth's **accolade.**

5. **décolletage**   (dā′ kôl täzh′)   [*de* <L. "from," "away from"]
   n. A low neckline on a garment or a garment with a low neckline.

   The drafty medieval castle discouraged **décolletage** on court dresses.

   décolleté, *adj.*

CORPUS, CORPORIS <L. "body"

6. **corporal**   (kôr′pə rəl)
   adj. Relating to or having an effect on the human body.

   In the nineteenth century **corporal** punishment usually meant "flogging": beating with a whip or stick.

   corporality, *n.*; **corporally,** *adv.*

7. **corporeal**   (kôr pôr′ē əl, kôr pō′rē əl)
adj. 1. Characteristic of or resembling the physical body.

The twins were identical in both **corporeal** and intellectual qualities.

2. Having material substance; able to be seen.

Was the ghost of Hamlet's father imaginary or **corporeal?**

corporeity, *n.*

8. **corps**   (kōr, kôr)
n. (plural) 1. A military organization of officers or of officers and enlistees.

The cadets of the U.S. Marine **Corps** saluted smartly.

2. An army unit.

During World War II the Women's Army **Corps** became known familiarly by its acronym, WACs.

3. A group of people having purpose and direction in common.

During dry months in the mountains a fire-fighting **corps** stays on alert.

9. **corpulent**   (kôr′pyə lənt)
adj. Excessively bulky; fat.

Some designers specialize in clothes to flatter the **corpulent** figure.

corpulence, *n.*; **corpulently,** *adv.*

10. **corpus**   (kôr′pəs)
n. 1. A body or collection of writings.

Some people believe that "Paul's Case" is the masterpiece of Willa Cather's **corpus** of short stories.

2. A structure of special character in an animal body.

Radiation destroyed the cancerous **corpus.**

COR, CORDIS <L. "heart"

11. **accord**   (ə kôrd′)   [*ac* = *ad* <L. "to," "toward"]
n. Harmony; agreement.

Her ambitions were not in **accord** with those of her parents.

<table>
<tr><td>

Familiar Words
according
accordingly
corsage
courage
discord
encourage
record

</td><td>

tr. v. To grant or bestow upon.

In 1797 New Jersey became the first state to **accord** voting rights to women.

intr. v. To agree.

Our plans for a picnic **accorded** well with the sunny weather.

</td></tr>
</table>

12. **cordial** (kôr′jəl)
   adj. 1. Hearty; warm; sincere.

   A **cordial** exchange of letters between the English poets Elizabeth Barrett and Robert Browning began the friendship that led to their marriage in 1846.

   2. Stimulating.

   The remodeled library is a **cordial** environment for study.

13. **concordance** (kən kôr′dəns) [*con = cum* <L. "with"]
   n. 1. A state of agreement; harmony.

   The heads of state achieved **concordance** through patient diplomacy.

   2. An alphabetical index of all the words in a text or corpus of texts, showing every occurrence of a word.

   The **concordance** to Shakespeare lets you track down any word or phrase used in his plays and poems.

   concord, *n.*; **concordant**, *adj.*

   NOTA BENE: *Kardia,* the Greek word for "heart," gives us *cardiac,* "pertaining to the heart." Other derivatives are *cardiologist, cardiology, cardiogram, hypocardium,* and *tachycardia.*

OS, OSSIS <L. "bone"

14. **ossify** (ŏs′ə fī′) [*-fy = facere* <L. "to make"]
   intr. v. 1. To turn into bone; to become bony.

   An infant's skull does not **ossify** fully until after birth.

   2. To become rigid (in behavior, habits, or beliefs).

   The theories of astronomers do not **ossify** because new data constantly change them.

   ossification, *n.*

NOTA BENE: *Os,* meaning "bone," shows that it is indebted to *osteon* <G. "bone," which provides these derivatives: *osteopath, osteology,* and *osteoporosis.*

You may have noticed that the first form of the Latin word for "mouth," *os, oris,* is identical to that of "bone," *os, ossis.* In each instance, *os* is the form used as the subject of a Latin sentence. Variations in word endings show the meaning just as context does. For example, in English, *plane* can mean either "airplane" or "level surface," depending on its context.

EXERCISE 11A   Circle the letter of the best SYNONYM (the word or phrase most nearly the same as the word in bold-faced type).

1. an author's **corpus**   a. remains   b. theme   c. collected work   d. library   e. body
2. a **carrion** bird   a. carnivorous   b. dead-flesh-eating   c. large   d. fighting   e. diseased
3. to receive **accolades**   a. blame   b. explanations   c. stimulants   d. praise   e. agreements
4. a graceful **décolletage**   a. decapitation   b. high collar   c. paper cut-out   d. necklace   e. low neckline

Circle the letter of the best ANTONYM (the word or phrase most nearly opposite the word in bold-faced type).

5. to **accord** recognition   a. withhold   b. bestow   c. expect   d. enjoy   e. resist
6. a(n) **corpulent** figure   a. important   b. muscular   c. tall   d. serious   e. slim
7. a(n) **corporal** wound   a. bodily   b. war   c. head   d. serious   e. imaginary
8. an enterprising **corps**   a. corporation   b. fire department   c. military unit   d. individual worker   e. committee
9. a(n) **ossified** attitude   a. respected   b. boring   c. ever-changing   d. solidifying   e. amusing

EXERCISE 11B   Circle the letter of the sentence in which the word in bold-faced type is used incorrectly

1. a. In medieval morality plays, human qualities appeared in **corporeal** form, such as a female character named "Good Deeds."
   b. Most states have banned **corporeal** punishment.

    c. Although blobs of paint had been blown on the canvas by an airplane propeller, viewers saw **corporeal** shapes.

    d. She claimed that the ghost first spoke to her and then became **corporeal.**

2. a. Because James Joyce's *Ulysses* is so complex, many students find it easier to read with the help of a **concordance.**

    b. Students need a **concordance** for checking definitions of words.

    c. After years of feuding in scholarly journals, the two scientists achieved **concordance** by writing a book together.

    d. The emissaries at the peace table struggled to find issues on which they were **concordant.**

3. a. The Battle of Waterloo was notorious for its **carnage.**

    b. Persistently harsh critics can cause **carnage** in literary and artistic circles.

    c. History books record **carnage** resulting from overzealously held prejudices.

    d. Their favorite dish is chili con **carnage.**

4. a. Maria Callas accepted the **accolades** of her enthusiastic fans at the opera's conclusion.

    b. The critic's bitter **accolade** enraged the playwright.

    c. The geneticist Barbara McClintock received a long-delayed **accolade** in 1983, the Nobel Prize in physiology or medicine.

    d. In Japan people outstanding for their creative work receive the **accolade** of being designated National Treasures.

5. a. My little sister is mischief **incarnate.**

    b. Albert Einstein represents the **incarnation** of scientific genius in the twentieth century.

    c. The philanthropist was a truly **incarnate** human being.

    d. The angels who defy God in John Milton's poem *Paradise Lost* make **incarnate** the idea of flagrant disobedience.

6. a. The enforcement of strict rules caused the children to consider their parents **ossified.**

    b. A person stops growing when the cartilage between the bones has **ossified.**

    c. The test of a chicken's age is the degree of **ossification** of its breastbone.

    d. After making clay bowls in ceramics class, we put them in the kiln to **ossify.**

EXERCISE 11C   Fill in each blank with the most appropriate word from Lesson 11. Use a
word or any of its forms only once.

1. Some Shakespearean scholars may not need a(n)

   _____ because they know every line from
   memory.

2. When a social group is isolated for a long time, customs tend to

   _____, making change difficult.

3. The buzzard hovered over the dying rabbit, intent on an imminent

   feast of _____.

4. The _____ of Charles Darwin's works has
   continued to be important to biologists for more than a century.

5. The noisy café was not a _____ environment
   for conversation.

6. To lose weight _____ people sometimes adopt
   a program of jogging or aerobics.

7. Known as the "Swedish Nightingale," Jenny Lind became the

   _____ representation of vocal brilliance in the
   nineteenth century.

8. Many veterans of the war in Vietnam find it hard to forget the

   _____ they witnessed.

LESSON 12

Summa sedes non capit duos.
The highest seat does not hold two
(i.e., There's room for only one at the top).

Key Words		
assiduous	dossier	gastronome
consanguinity	endorse	sanguine
dermatology	enervate	seance
dissident	epidermis	sedentary
dorsal	gastric	supersede

DERMA <G. "skin"

1. **dermatology** (dûr′ mə tŏl′ə jē) [*logos* <G. "word," "speech," "thought"]
   n. The scientific study of the skin and its diseases.

   An allergic reaction of the skin is one of the concerns of **dermatology.**

   dermatologist, *n.*

2. **epidermis** (ĕp′ ə dûr′ mĭs) [*epi* <G. "over"]
   n. The outer protective layer of the skin or outer layer of various organisms. (In plants, the outer layer of cells.)

   The hunter's arrow did not puncture the elephant's thick **epidermis.**

   epidermal, *adj.*; **epidermic,** *adj.*

DORSUM <L. "the back"

3. **dorsal** (dôr′səl)
   adj. Pertaining to the back, especially of animals.

   When the **dorsal** fin of the shark rose from the water, swimmers fled.

4. **dossier** (dŏs′ē ā, dôs′yā)
   n. A set of documents containing information about a person or event; a file.

   The candidate for a federal judgeship submitted a thick **dossier.**

5. **endorse** (ĕn dôrs′, ĭn dôrs′) [*en* = *in* <L. "on"]
   tr. v. 1. To write one's signature on the back of a check or other document.

   Banks require that payees **endorse** a check within a specified space.

   2. To sign a contract.

   Both parties must **endorse** the contract to make it binding.

   3. To acknowledge receipt of payment.

   The cashier **endorsed** the check by stamping it "Paid."

   4. To support actively; to sanction.

   In 1969 the Labor Party in Israel **endorsed** Golda Meir as prime minister, a position she held until 1974.

   endorsee, *n.*; **endorsement,** *n.*

GASTER, GASTREROS (also GASTROS) <G. "stomach," "belly"

6. **gastric**   (găs′ trĭk)
   adj. Pertaining to the stomach.

   Gastric juices are acidic.

7. **gastronome**   (găs′ trə nōm)
   n. A person who is knowledgeable about good food and drink; a gourmet.

   In decades of writing about food, M. F. K. Fisher proved herself an elegant writer as well as a **gastronome.**

NERVUS <L. "sinew," "nerve"

8. **enervate**   (ĕn′ ər vāt′)   [*e = ex* <L. "from," "out of"]
   tr. v. To deprive of strength; to weaken.

   The heavy lunch **enervated** us.

   NOTA BENE: The Greek word for "nerve" is *neuron*. Derivatives from *neuron* are *neural, neurology, neurosis,* and *neurosurgeon.*

SANGUIS, SANGUINIS <L. "blood"

9. **sanguine**   (săng′ gwĭn)
   adj. 1. Cheerful; hopeful.

   The baseball team remained **sanguine** despite their losing season.

   2. Reddish or ruddy.

   Her complexion was **sanguine,** as if she had just returned from skiing.

   sanguinary, *adj.*; **sanguinity,** *n.*

   NOTA BENE: In the Middle Ages, people were classified according to four groups of "humors" or temperaments, determined by fluids in the body: *sanguine* (blood), "cheerful"; *phlegmatic* (phlegm), "sluggish"; *choleric* (yellow bile), "easily angered"; and *melancholy* (black bile), "gloomy."

10. **consanguinity** (kŏn′ săng gwĭn′ ə tē)   [*con* = *cum* <L. "with"]
     n. 1. Blood relationship.

     Although the four sisters in Louisa May Alcott's *Little Women* enjoy **consanguinity,** they differ greatly in temperament.

     2. Any close relationship.

     A feeling of **consanguinity** often develops from being classmates for several years.

     consanguineous, *adj.*

     NOTA BENE: Greek as well as Latin words from "blood" have entered English. *Haima* <G. "blood" provides *hemoglobin, hemophilia, hemophobia,* and *hemorrhage.*
          Other words related to the body come from *pneuma* <G. "breath," "spirit": *pneumatic, pneumonia, pneumograph,* and *pneumogastric.* From *pleumon* <G. "lung" and *pulmo, pulmonis* <L. "lung" comes *pulmonary.*

Familiar Words
assess
hostage
preside
president
resident
residue
sediment
session
sewer
siege
subsidize
subsidy

Challenge Words
obsession
presidium
sessile

SEDEO, SEDERE, SEDI, SESSUM <L. "to sit," "to settle"

11. **assiduous** (ə sĭj′ o͞o əs)   [*as* = *ad* <L. "to," "toward"]
     adj. 1. Unceasingly attentive; devoted.

     Freshwater aquariums require **assiduous** care.

     2. Persistent; diligent.

     Winners of the national spelling contest have been **assiduous** in learning how to spell unusual words.

     assiduity, *n.*

12. **dissident** (dĭs′ ə dənt)   [*dis* <L. "away from," "apart"]
     adj. Differing; disagreeing; dissenting.

     Totalitarian governments do not tolerate **dissident** voices.

     n. A person who disagrees.

     A group of **dissidents** was arrested for protesting the possession of firearms by private citizens.

     dissidence, *n.*

13. **seance** (sā′ äns′)
     n. A meeting at which a spiritualist attempts to communicate with the dead.

     At the **seance,** no communication came from the other world.

14. **sedentary** (sĕd′n tĕr′ ē)

    adj. 1. Characterized by much sitting.

    Computer programmers spend many **sedentary** hours at their desks.

    2. Remaining in one area; not migratory.

    Giving up herding for agriculture, the tribes became **sedentary** and cities arose.

15. **supersede** (soo′ pər sēd′) [*super* <L. "above"]

    tr. v. To take the place of; to replace.

    The steamship **superseded** the sailing ship as the standard ocean-going vessel.

EXERCISE 12A

Circle the letter of the best SYNONYM (the word or phrase most nearly the same as the word in bold-faced type).

1. to **endorse** a philanthropic cause   a. support   b. organize
   c. sign a contract for   d. pay for   e. denounce
2. a spiny **epidermis**   a. back   b. neck   c. outer layer of skin
   d. inner layer of skin   e. chest
3. a job keeping one **sedentary**   a. seated   b. bored   c. orderly
   d. active   e. standing

Circle the letter of the best ANTONYM (the word or phrase most nearly opposite the word in bold-faced type).

4. **enervated** by jet lag   a. made nervous   b. energized   c. weakened
   d. made hungry   e. disturbed
5. to **supersede** the mayor   a. retain   b. replace   c. reject   d. honor
   e. precede
6. **assiduous** nurses   a. dedicated   b. weary   c. careless   d. clever
   e. energetic

EXERCISE 12B

Circle the letter of the sentence in which the word in bold-faced type is used incorrectly.

1. a. Chewing gum stimulates the flow of **gastric** juices.
   b. Sometimes **gastric** pain frightens people into mistaking it for cardiac pain.

    c. Scarlet **gastric** bands are highly fashionable this year.

    d. A **gastric** ailment blights the pleasures of a gastronome.

2. a. **Dissidents** historically had difficulty in obtaining visas allowing them to emigrate from the Soviet Union.

    b. Our seats were so **dissident** that we could barely see each other across the auditorium.

    c. The city council meetings became lively when **dissidents** protested the increase in parking fees.

    d. Our teacher encouraged **dissidence** when we discussed election issues.

3. a. The genealogist looks for lines of **consanguinity.**

    b. His **consanguinity** made him the life of the party.

    c. The two eldest Bennet sisters in Jane Austen's novel *Pride and Prejudice* express **consanguinity** of both blood and spirit.

    d. Although the twins had been separated at birth, tests proved their **consanguinity.**

4. a. The lumberjack injured a **dorsal** muscle in his chest.

    b. Scorpion fish attack their victims with poisonous **dorsal** spines.

    c. The closeness of **dorsal** nerves to the spinal column makes back surgery difficult.

    d. The camel with a single **dorsal** hump is called a dromedary.

5. a. Completing **dossiers** for college admission requires much time.

    b. The FBI had compiled a detailed **dossier** on the suspected spy.

    c. Several lumpy objects strained the fabric of the **dossier** strapped to the cyclist's back.

    d. The personnel director scrutinized the applicant's **dossier.**

6. a. Charles Dickens's character Mr. Micawber is continually **sanguine,** always expecting that "something will turn up."

    b. Eyeing the **sanguine** evening sky, the sailor predicted good weather for the next day.

    c. **Sanguine** and ermine are furs favored by European royalty.

    d. The exertion of the marathon brought a **sanguine** glow to the runners' faces.

7. a. The calligrapher always **endorses** checks with a flourish.

    b. The forger was caught **endorsing** the bill of sale with the bank president's name.

    c. American political parties are increasingly **endorsing** women candidates for high office.

    d. Some athletes lift weights to **endorse** their muscles.

8. a. The serious gardener is **assiduous** in pulling weeds.

    b. **Assiduous** trees lose their leaves in autumn.

    c. Because of the treasurer's **assiduity,** the group's financial records were always in order.

    d. Human beings are unconsciously **assiduous** in forgetting things that are too painful to remember.

9. a. Some automobile owners **supersede** their cars annually.
   b. The tractor has **superseded** the ox and plow on American farms.
   c. In some organizations the vice-president automatically **supersedes** the president.
   d. Popular music fans are often fickle as one idol quickly **supersedes** another.

EXERCISE 12C   Fill in each blank with the most appropriate word from Lesson 12. Use a word or any of its forms only once.

1. Climbing at altitudes where oxygen is thin can _____ hikers very quickly.

2. Julia Child's reputation as a(n) _____ was established when she first demonstrated gourmet cooking on television.

3. The painter caught the _____ flush of youthful embarrassment.

4. An expert in _____ gave a lecture on skin disease.

5. Bank tellers expect you to _____ checks legibly.

6. During the _____ the listeners thought they heard their dead grandfather tap the table three times.

7. Software developers, judges, and professional writers engage in _____ occupations.

8. Dinosaurs known as spinosaurids developed overgrown backbones that are called _____ "sails."

9. Many Hollywood actors lost their livelihoods as talking pictures _____ silent films.

10. The human _____, no thicker than a sheet of paper, contains both dead and living cells.

REVIEW EXERCISES FOR LESSONS 11 AND 12

1 Circle the letter of the best answer to the following analogies and questions about roots and definitions.

1. dermatology : skin : :
   a. carrion : heart
   b. ossification : back

LESSONS 11 AND 12: THE BODY

    c. seance : chair

    d. gastronomy : stomach

    e. incarnation : nerve

2. assiduity : laziness : :

    a. seance : carnage

    b. concordance : dissidence

    c. corpus : consanguinity

    d. cordiality : décolletage

    e. concordance : ossification

3. concordance : words and phrases : :

    a. dossier : accolades

    b. corpulence : gastronomes

    c. corpus : written works

    d. carnage : carrion

    e. consanguinity : cordiality

4. Which word is defined incorrectly?

    a. décolletage — "low neckline"

    b. accord — "agreement"

    c. carnage — "massacre"

    d. endorse — "to back down"

    e. enervate — "to deprive of strength"

5. Which English word is *not* a derivative of the Latin or Greek word that follows it?

    a. epidermis — *derma*

    b. affront — *frons*

    c. supersede — *os*

    d. seance — *sedere*

    e. corporal — *corpus*

6. Which pair of words is the only set derived from words related to internal organs of the body?

    a. sanguine — incarnate

    b. cordial — gastric

    c. sedentary — epidermis

    d. dorsal — ossified

    e. enervated — corporeal

2 Substitute the appropriate word from Lessons 11 or 12 for each word or phrase in parentheses in the following paragraphs. No word is used more than once.

1. In his *Theory of the Leisure Class*, sociologist Thorstein Veblen describes how the eighteenth-century working partnership of

   husbands and wives was _____ (replaced) in the nineteenth century by the non-working, middle-class wife whose

   leisure was _____ (bestowed) by her

husband's economic success. For some middle-class women, this circumscribed lifestyle led to the development of pastimes that were _____ (characterized by much sitting), such as embroidery, drawing, music, and reading. Confinement to a strictly domestic life _____ (weakened) and frustrated other women, who longed for education and a meaningful role in political and professional life. However, most working-class women sought to imitate the manners and values of women who did not have to work.

2. American ethnologist Jane Goodall has received many

_____ (honors) for her _____ (unceasingly persistent) efforts to improve the lives of both human beings and animals in Tanzania, where she has lived and worked for many years. In 1991 she founded the program Roots and Shoots to encourage conservation among schoolchildren in village schools throughout Tanzania. She has received enthusiastic

_____ (support) for her powerful opposition to the _____ (massive slaughter) of wild animals.

3 Writing or Discussion Activities

1. Write a sentence for each of the following words, describing yourself or someone you know in the act of being
   a. assiduous.
   b. cordial.
   c. sanguine.
   d. enervated.
2. Have you had a personal possession that once meant a great deal to you but has now been replaced by something else? Write a sentence in which you use the verb *supersede* and identify the possession(s).
3. To what extent are you a *gastronome*? Write a paragraph showing with specific examples the degree to which you are or are not "one who practices the art or science of good eating."
4. What skill, talent, characteristic, or accomplishment do you possess that you have reason to be proud of? Write an *accolade* about yourself, giving reasons for deserving praise. Or if you prefer, write an *accolade* about someone else, a person you sincerely admire. Include specific details.

The Hands

LESSON 13

Manus manum fricat, et manus manum lavat.
Hand rubs hand, and hand washes hand
(an illustration of mutual assistance).—PROVERB

Key Words		
ambidextrous	genuflect	manipulate
deflect	inflection	rapacious
dexterity	manacle	rapt
digital	mandate	reflection
emancipate	manifest	surreptitious

MANUS <L. "hand"

1. **emancipate** (ĭ măn′ sə pāt′) [*e* = *ex* <L. "from," "out of"]
tr. v. 1. To free from restraint or influence.

The nineteenth amendment to the U.S. Constitution **emancipated** women as voters in 1920.

2. To free (a slave) from bondage.

President Lincoln issued in 1863 an edict to **emancipate** slaves.

emancipation, *n.*

2. **manacle**   (măn′ə kəl)
   n. (usually plural) 1. A device for confining the hands; handcuffs.

   Their **manacles** were removed, and the prisoners were set free.

   2. Anything that constrains.

   With consistent practice one can throw off the **manacles** of insecurity as a public speaker.

   tr. v. To restrain, as with manacles.

   Lack of money has **manacled** many projects to improve roads and public transportation.

3. **mandate**   (măn′dāt)
   n. A formal order from a higher court; an authoritative command, order, or injunction.

   A court of appeals **mandate** overturned the verdict of the district court.

4. **manifest**   (măn′ə fĕst′)   [*festus* <L. "gripped"]
   adj. Clearly apparent to sight or understanding; obvious.

   Although Helen Keller was blind and deaf from age two, her intelligence became **manifest** through the patience and skill of her teacher, Anne Sullivan.

   tr. v. 1. To show plainly; to reveal.

   After months in the Tropics the travelers **manifested** the symptoms of malaria.

   2. To prove.

   Her birth certificate **manifests** her American citizenship.

   n. A list of cargo or passengers.

   Check the **manifest** to see if a doctor is on board.

   manifestation, *n.*; **manifestly,** *adv.*; **manifesto,** *n.*

5. **manipulate**   (mə nĭp′yə lāt)   [*manipulus* <L. "handful"]
   tr. v. 1. To use or handle skillfully.

   After learning in high school how to **manipulate** stage lights on cue, she went on to a career in theatrical lighting.

   2. To manage with devious skill, or to adjust to suit one's purpose.

Queen Elizabeth I of England cleverly **manipulated** her royal suitors, pretending interest in marriage as a way to maintain peace with their countries.

manipulation, *n.*; **manipulative,** *adj.*

> **Challenge Words**
> digitalis
> digitigrade
> prestidigitation

DEXTRA <L. "right hand"

6. **dexterity** (dĕk stĕr′ ə tē)
   n. 1. Skill in the use of the hands or body; adroitness.

   The **dexterity** of the jugglers was manifest as balls, then knives, and then flaming torches kept flying over their heads.

   2. Mental skill or adroitness; cleverness.

   The complexity of computer programs shows the **dexterity** of their designers.

   dexterous or **dextrous,** *adj.*

7. **ambidextrous** (am′ bĭ dĕk′strəs) [*ambi* <L. "on both sides"]
   adj. Able to use either hand equally well.

   The **ambidextrous** pitcher kept batters off balance.

   ambidexter, *n.*; **ambidexterity,** *n.*

DIGITUS <L. "finger"

8. **digital** (dĭj′ə təl)
   adj. 1. Relating to a finger or to a unit of measure ($^{3}/_{4}$ inch) the breadth of a finger.

   Lacemaking requires exceptional **digital** skill.

   2. Referring to a numerical system for encoding data.

   Digital recordings capture fine distinctions in sound.

   digit, *n.*

   NOTA BENE: The Greek word for "finger" is *daktulos,* which can also mean "toe" and "digit." It adds to English the words *dactylic,* referring to a three-syllable unit, or "foot," in poetry (the first syllable is stressed and the others are unstressed); and *pterodactyl,* an extinct flying reptile having an elongated digit on each forelimb.

Familiar Words
flex
flexible
inflexible
reflector
reflex

Challenge Words
flexure
reflexive

FLECTO, FLECTERE, FLEXI, FLEXUM
<L. "to bend"

9. **deflect**   (dĭ flĕkt′)   [*de* <L. "from," "away from"]
    tr. v. To turn aside.

    The official tried to **deflect** the reporter's embarrassing questions.

    intr. v. To swerve or turn aside.

    The rocket **deflected** from its course and exploded seconds after firing.

    deflection, *n.*

10. **genuflect**   (jĕn′ yə flĕkt′)   [*genu* <L. "knee"]
    intr. v. 1. To bend the knee in a kneeling or half-kneeling position to express reverence or respect.

    King Richard II chided the Duke of Northumberland for failing to **genuflect,** an honor due the English monarch.

    genuflection, *n.*

11. **inflection**   (ĭn flĕk′shən)   [*in* <L. "in"]
    n. 1. An alteration of pitch or tone of the voice.

    The English often ask questions with a falling **inflection;** Americans, with a rising **inflection.**

    2. In grammar, an alteration of the form of a word to show different grammatical or syntactical relationships.

    The second-person pronoun *you* has no **inflection,** but the third-person pronouns *we, our,* and *us* are inflected forms.

    inflect, *v.;* **inflected,** *adj.*

12. **reflection**   (rĭ flĕk′shən)   [*re* <L. "back," "again"]
    n. 1. The act or condition of being thrown back.

    Their good manners were a **reflection** of a genteel upbringing.

    2. Something thrown back, as light, heat, sound, or an image.

    The breeze over the pond blurred the **reflection** of autumn foliage.

    3. Discredit; indirect reproach.

    His inability to share is a **reflection** on his character.

4. Deep thought.

Isak Dinesen's book, *Out of Africa,* includes **reflections** about Africa and her life there.

reflect, *v.*; **reflective,** *adj.*

RAPIO, RAPERE, RAPUI, RAPTUM <L. "to snatch"

> **Familiar Words**
> enraptured
> rapid
> rapids
> rapture
> ravenous

13. **rapacious**   (rə pā′shəs)
    adj. 1. Excessively grasping or greedy.

    Rapacious land developers endangered the wildlife preserve.

    2. Given to seizing for plunder or as prey.

    Rapacious slave traders destroyed flourishing kingdoms in Africa.

    rapacity, *n.*

> **Challenge Words**
> rapine
> ravine
> ravish

14. **rapt**   (răpt)
    adj. 1. Giving one's complete attention.

    The storyteller held the children in **rapt** silence as they listened to the adventures of Brer Rabbit.

    2. Overcome with emotion; completely filled with joy.

    The **rapt** gaze that Romeo and Juliet exchange signifies love at first sight.

    raptly, *adv.*; **raptness,** *n.*

15. **surreptitious**   (sûr′ əp tĭsh′ əs)   [*sur = sub* <L. "under"]
    adj. Done secretly, without approval.

    Our **surreptitious** raids on the cookie jar ended when we got caught.

    surreptitiously, *adv.*; **surreptitiousness,** *n.*

EXERCISE 13A   Circle the letter of the best SYNONYM (the word or phrase most nearly the same as the word in bold-faced type).

1. eager to **manipulate** an opponent   a. fight   b. encourage
   c. challenge   d. influence   e. pounce upon
2. a prisoner in **manacles**   a. gloves   b. handcuffs   c. overalls
   d. spectacles   e. leg restraints

3. a pleasing **inflection**   a. modulation of voice   b. choice of words
   c. pronunciation   d. understanding of grammar   e. volume
4. to **genuflect** reverently   a. pray   b. bend at the knee   c. bow from
   the waist   d. nod the head   e. remove a hat
5. a **mandate** to change policy   a. chance   b. requirement
   c. refusal   d. device   e. stimulus

Circle the letter of the best ANTONYM (the word or phrase most nearly
opposite the word in bold-faced type).

6. **dexterity** with tools   a. right-handedness   b. care   c. accuracy
   d. adroitness   e. clumsiness
7. to **manifest** confidence   a. ascertain   b. hold   c. hint at
   d. conceal   e. measure
8. **rapt** in thought   a. uninvolved   b. transported   c. deep
   d. enclosed   e. rambling
9. a **surreptitious** act   a. fraudulent   b. repetitious
   c. straightforward   d. secret   e. silly
10. **rapacious** carnivores   a. ferocious   b. cruel   c. shy
    d. silent   e. greedy

EXERCISE 13B

Circle the letter of the sentence in which the word in bold-faced type is
used incorrectly.

1. a. My refusal to eat dessert is not a **reflection** on your cooking.
   b. Their prejudice was a **reflection** of their ignorance.
   c. The French writer Montaigne developed the habit of writing
      down his **reflections** and thereby invented the genre we know as
      the essay.
   d. Leaping from the springboard, the diver performed three
      complete **reflections** before entering the water.
2. a. The **manifest** listed all of the passengers on the ship except one:
      the stowaway.
   b. The cook **manifested** a delicious lunch, including lemon mousse.
   c. That Lady Astor and Sir Winston Churchill detested each other
      was **manifested** by their exchange of witty insults.
   d. Her mechanical skill was **manifest** when she built a rocket.
3. a. The children **mandated** that their guests wear costumes to the
      birthday party.
   b. In 1954 a U.S. Supreme Court's **mandate** outlawed segregation
      and separate-but-equal education in public schools.
   c. The electorate gave their senator a **mandate** to oppose capital
      punishment.
   d. My parents issued a **mandate:** "Always wear your bicycle helmet!"

4. a. Doctors recommend **digital** exercises for arthritis sufferers.
   b. Improved technology makes possible increasing fidelity in the new **digital** recordings.
   c. Pianists must develop strength in their little **digitals.**
   d. The typist's **digital** nimbleness impressed his supervisors.

5. a. A public speaker must be attentive to **inflection,** pace, and volume.
   b. Changing "I say" to "he or she says" illustrates English **inflection.**
   c. Vocal **inflection** of Japanese differs greatly from that of American English.
   d. She tried to enhance her life with **inflections** of culture.

6. a. Fans of Richard Wagner listen **raptly** to the soaring operatic duet of lovers Elsa and Lohengrin.
   b. When Macbeth hears the witches' prediction of "royal hope" in Act I of Shakespeare's play, Banquo observes that his friend "seems **rapt.**"
   c. The Egyptian mummy had been carefully **rapt** in fine linen.
   d. In a hypnotic trance, the **rapt** patient could recall details of her earliest childhood.

7. a. Jane Austen wrote her novels **surreptitiously,** covering the manuscripts at every knock on the door.
   b. One reaches a destination faster on a **surreptitious** underground train than on a bus contending with traffic.
   c. In 1605 Guy Fawkes **surreptitiously** stored gunpowder under the Houses of Parliament, plotting to blow them up.
   d. General Washington's **surreptitious** crossing of the Delaware River on Christmas night, 1776, allowed a successful assault on British troops.

8. a. People in every culture try to **emancipate** themselves from hampering stereotypes.
   b. Women achieved **emancipation** in dress with the shorter, looser clothing of the 1920s.
   c. Richard Wright learned that books could **emancipate** him from restrictions posed by Southern culture.
   d. Gloves are a useful way to **emancipate** unsightly hands.

EXERCISE 13C

Fill in each blank with the most appropriate word from Lesson 13. Use a word or any of its forms only once.

1. Playing with blocks helps children develop _____ coordination.

2. Because she is _____ she can do her homework even with her dominant arm in a cast.

3. After she spilled her coffee, the embarrassed guest tried

   to _____ attention from herself.

4. Georgia O'Keeffe's glowing paintings of adobe houses, rock

   formations, and mesas _____ her love of the
   Southwest.

5. The new employee almost _____ whenever
   his boss is present.

6. Some organizations stress the idea that an individual's behavior is

   a(n) _____ of the group's standards.

7. The jackal is a(n) _____ hunter, not only
   tracking live animals, but also feeding on carrion.

LESSON 14

Manu propria.
With one's own hands (a phrase medieval artists used to assert
that no apprentice had helped in their work).

Key Words

apprehend	explicate	ploy
complicity	explicit	ply
comprise	exploit	reprehend
duplicity	imply	reprisal
entrepreneur	impregnable	supplicate

Familiar Words
accomplice
apply
complex
comply
display
duplex
duplicate
employ
multiply
pliant
plight
supply
triplicate

PLICO, PLICARE, PLICAVI, PLICATUM <L. "to fold"

1. **complicity**   (kəm plĭs′ə tē)   [*com* = *cum* <L. "with"]
   n. Participation with another in an act that is or seems to be
   deceitful.

   Complicity of Mary Queen of Scots in a plan to murder Queen
   Elizabeth I appears in letters written in 1586.

2. **duplicity**   (dōō plĭs′ə tē)   [*duo* <L. "two"]
   n. 1. Deceitfulness in speech or conduct; double-dealing.

   Voters do not approve of **duplicity** by elected officials.

   2. Being physically or numerically double or two-fold; doubleness.

Challenge Words
deploy
implicate
multiplex
multiplicity
plissé
replicate

The computer works with a binary system, a basic **duplicity** of numbers—*0* and *1*.

3. **explicate**   (ĕks′plĭ kāt)   [*ex* <L. "from," "out of"]
   tr. v. To make clear; to explain thoroughly, often in a literary context.

   If you are reading a novel such as *Madame Bovary* in your French class, your teacher will no doubt ask you to **explicate** the text.

   explicable, *adj.*; **explication,** *n.*; **explicative,** *adj.*

4. **explicit**   (ĕk splĭs′ĭt, ĕk splĭs′ ət)   [*ex* <L. "from," "out of"]
   adj. Definite; stated in detail, leaving nothing to be guessed at; outspoken.

   When giving directions, be **explicit.**

   Antonym: **implicit.**

5. **exploit**   (ĕks′ploit′)   [*ex* <L. "from," "out of"]
   n. A notable or heroic deed.

   English-born aviator Beryl Markham's greatest **exploit** was making the first solo flight from east to west across the Atlantic Ocean.

   (ĕks ploit′)   *tr. v.* 1. To use to the greatest advantage.

   Eleanor Roosevelt **exploited** her position as First Lady to express herself on human rights issues.

   2. To make use of selfishly or unethically.

   Some authors write books that **exploit** their association with famous people.

   3. To publicize.

   The billboard **exploited** the long run of *Les Misérables* on Broadway.

   exploitable, *adj.*; **exploitation,** *n.*; **exploiter,** *n.*

6. **imply**   (ĭm plī′)   [*im* = *in* <L. "in"]
   tr. v. 1. To indicate indirectly; to hint.

   Although no longer a girl herself, Margot Fonteyn could **imply** lovestruck adolescence when she danced in the ballet *Romeo and Juliet.*

   NOTA BENE: *Imply* often refers to what a speaker says; this verb is sometimes confused with *infer,* which refers to the listener's response to what is implied. Examples: My teacher *implied* that I had done well. I *inferred* from my teacher's tone of voice that I had done well.

   2. To require as a necessary condition.

Cooperative development projects **imply** a condition of peaceful coexistence among nations.

implication, *n.*

7. **ploy**　(ploi)
   n. A tactic intended to frustrate, embarrass, or gain an advantage over an opponent.

   The tennis player's constant chatter may be a **ploy** to disrupt a rival's concentration.

8. **ply**　(plī)
   tr. v. 1. To use a tool or weapon vigorously; to work at a trade.

   The quiltmakers talked and sang as they **plied** their needles and thread.

   2. To offer something persistently.

   Our teachers **ply** us with questions to make us think.

   n. 1. The thickness of cloth, yarn, or rope.

   You will need rope of a thicker **ply** to secure the anchor.

   2. Wood layered with crosswise grain.

   Wood with **ply** has double strength.

9. **supplicate**　(sŭp′lĭ kāt)　[*sup = sub* <L. "under"]
   tr. v. To ask humbly or earnestly for, as in praying; to beseech.

   When the legendary Greek women warriors, the Amazons, were in difficulty, they **supplicated** the goddess Artemis.

   suppliant, *n.*; **supplicant,** *n.*; **supplication,** *n.*

PREHENDO, PREHENDERE, PREHENDI, PREHENSUM
<L. "to catch," "to seize," "to grasp"

10. **apprehend**　(ăp′rĭ hĕnd′)　[*ap = ad* <L. "to," "toward"]
    tr. v. 1. To arrest.

    The police **apprehended** the thieves carrying stolen goods.

    2. To grasp mentally; to understand.

    Albert Einstein's theory of relativity is difficult to **apprehend** because it combines complex elements of physics and mathematics.

    3. To anticipate with anxiety.

    The intense competition for places makes high school students in Japan **apprehend** the difficult university entrance examinations.

apprehensible, *adj.*; **apprehension,** *n.*; **apprehensive,** *adj.*

11. **comprise**   (kəm prīz′)   [*com* = *cum* <L. "with"]
    tr. v. 1. To consist of; to contain.

    The jury that found the defendant not guilty **comprised** six women and six men.

    > NOTE BENE: Careful writers guard against using *comprise* as a synonym for *compose*. *Comprise* is appropriate when the subject of the sentence, a general term, is followed by a listing of all the parts. Also note that *comprise* is not followed by *of* in passive voice.

12. **entrepreneur**   (än trə prə nûr′)   [*entre* <French "between" from *intro* = *in* <L. "between," "in"]
    n. A person who organizes, operates, and assumes the risk for business ventures.

    The lemonade stand was our first venture as **entrepreneurs.**

13. **impregnable**   (ĭm prĕg′nə bəl)   [*im* = *in* <L. "not"]
    adj. Strong enough to resist attack of capture, as a fortress.

    In World War II the French believed their Maginot Line to be **impregnable.**

    2. Not to be outweighed or overcome in argument.

    Confirmed Marxists regard their theories as **impregnable.**

14. **reprehend**   (rĕp rĭ hĕnd′)   [*re* <L. "back," "again"]
    tr. v. To reprimand, reprove, or express disapproval.

    The judge **reprehended** the attorney for manipulating the evidence.

    reprehensible, *adj.*; **reprehension,** *n.*

15. **reprisal**   (rĕ prī′zəl)   [*re* <L. "back," "again"]
    n. An action or act of retaliation against someone for injuries received.

    In 1942 the Nazis totally destroyed the Czechoslovakian village of Lidice as **reprisal** for the assassination of a German police official.

EXERCISE 14A   Circle the letter of the best SYNONYM (the word or phrase most nearly the same as the word in bold-faced type).

1. to be a successful **entrepreneur**   a. magician   b. undertaker
   c. translator   d. businessperson   e. animal trainer
2. to **ply** with food   a. supply eagerly   b. stuff   c. play   d. be stingy
   e. trick
3. to **supplicate** the queen   a. support   b. praise   c. reproach
   d. beseech   e. attack
4. behavior that **implies** obedience   a. suggests   b. demonstrates
   c. pretends   d. disdains   e. infers
5. a play **comprising** three acts   a. dramatizing   b. compressing
   c. containing   d. presenting   e. ruining

Circle the letter of the best ANTONYM (the word or phrase most nearly opposite the word in bold-faced type).

6. to **explicate** a paragraph   a. criticize   b. translate   c. misinterpret
   d. explain   e. read
7. to **reprehend** an offender   a. praise   b. rebuke   c. catch   d. hate
   e. release
8. a rival's **duplicity**   a. double-dealing   b. treachery   c. singularity
   d. ambidextrousness   e. fair play

EXERCISE 14B   Circle the letter of the sentence in which the word in bold-faced type is used incorrectly.

1. a. Because the enthusiastic audience called for a **reprisal,** the
      chorus sang another medley of ballads.
   b. The rapacious warriors expected **reprisal** following their attack.
   c. "Turning the other cheek" is the opposite response to **reprisal** for
      a victim of a wrong.
   d. Losing the title by one point, the team swore **reprisals** next
      season.
2. a. Just because Lillian Hellman **implied** familiarity with Communist
      theory, can you infer that she was a Communist?
   b. Downcast eyes and blushing **imply** shyness.
   c. Since 1952, hospitals have used Virginia Apgar's system of testing
      newborn babies to **imply** their degree of health.
   d. The design of Shaker furniture **implies** masterly artisans.
3. a. The players admitted **complicity** in losing the game on purpose.
   b. The spy acknowledged **complicity** in leaking classified
      information.
   c. Tom Sawyer draws Huck Finn into **complicity** to free Jim, who has
      already been declared a freed slave.

    d. Although poor, the family lived in cheerful, wholesome **complicity.**

4. a. The anguished parents **supplicated** the judge not to send their child to prison.
    b. The workers almost **supplicated** when the ladder collapsed under them.
    c. The committee **supplicated** corporations for donations.
    d. The young peasant girl, Joan of Arc, **supplicated** the Dauphin of France to allow her to lead the French army to victory.

5. a. The police were able to **apprehend** the culprits because they left fingerprints.
    b. The champion instantly **apprehended** the chess move required to put the challenger in check.
    c. Gazing up at the precipice, the climber **apprehended** the danger.
    d. Losing their balance in the tree, the children **apprehended** to the nearest branches.

6. a. Stephen Potter's book on "one-upmanship" describes **ploys** for getting the better of one's acquaintances.
    b. Expert anglers have **ploys** to outwit the wariest fish.
    c. A mechanical **ploy** fascinated the children at the toy store.
    d. Political actions sometimes begin as a **ploy** but grow into duplicity, as the Watergate affair in 1972 illustrated.

7. a. The weaver's best results came with using three-**ply** yarn.
    b. Cornelia Otis Skinner **plies** her readers with humorous travel situations in *Our Hearts Were Young and Gay.*
    c. The graduate **plied** for a job at the civic center.
    d. The cobbler had **plied** his trade for sixty years.

8. a. Some viewers protested the **explicit** language in the film.
    b. Our parents were **explicit** in designating our chores.
    c. My assignment was to **explicit** the sonnet.
    d. Thomas Hardy's description of the market town of Casterbridge is so **explicit** that the reader can draw a map of it.

EXERCISE 14C   Fill in each blank with the most appropriate word from Lesson 14. Use a word or any of its forms only once.

1. The film showing open heart surgery was so _____ that some students felt faint.

2. One of the _____ of Hercules in accomplishing his twelve labors was cleaning the vast Augean stables in one day.

3. Rachel Carson forcefully _____ the dangers of pesticides in her book *Silent Spring.*

4. The teacher _____ the student for using a cellular phone in class.

5. The Bill of Rights _____ ten articles, which are the first ten amendments to the U.S. Constitution.

6. Although medieval fortresses could withstand most attacks, they were not _____ when subjected to cannon fire.

7. Robert Louis Stevenson's characters Dr. Jekyll and Mr. Hyde represent the _____ of personality that can exist within a single person.

8. To take "an eye for an eye and a tooth for a tooth" is an act of _____.

9. So clearly did Helen Hunt Jackson _____ the plight of Native Americans in California that in 1884 she wrote a book about them.

REVIEW EXERCISES FOR LESSONS 13 AND 14

1 Circle the letter of the best answer to the following analogies and questions about roots and definitions.

1. genuflect : knee : :
   a. manacle : arm
   b. digital : wrist
   c. manifest : hand
   d. entrepreneur : finger
   e. inflection : voice
2. manifest : demonstrate : :
   a. supplicate : deceive
   b. explicate : confuse
   c. mandate : imply
   d. ply : deflect
   e. reprehend : disapprove
3. *manus* : *digitus* : :
   a. hand : foot
   b. foot : toe
   c. eye : ear
   d. knee : elbow
   e. hand : wrist

4. bend : fold : :
   a. *prehendere* : *digitus*
   b. *flectere* : *plicare*
   c. *plicare* : *flectere*
   d. *daktulos* : *flectere*
   e. *rapere* : *prehendere*

5. Which of these words is defined incorrectly?
   a. rapt — "uninterested"
   b. manacled — "hampered"
   c. deflected — "turned aside"
   d. dextrous — "skillful"
   e. rapacious — "greedy"

6. Which word is not derived from *plicare* or *prehendere*?
   a. impregnable
   b. imply
   c. reprisal
   d. entrepreneur
   e. surreptitious

2

Substitute the appropriate word from Lessons 13 or 14 for each word or phrase in parentheses in the following paragraphs. No word is used more than once.

1. Beginning his career as an eight-year-old circus performer, Harry Houdini by age twenty-eight was renowned as the world's most ________________________ (adroit) escape artist. Performing before thousands of ________________________ (transfixed) spectators, Houdini proved that he could extricate himself from ________________________ (handcuffs) and chains even when he was locked in boxes under water. No barrier or obstacle was ________________________ (unbreachable) for him.

2. Before the sale of medications came under United States government regulation, patent-medicine sellers were a familiar feature of American rural life. These "snake oil salesmen" ________________________ (took advantage of) gullible country people who had little access to medical care. One well-known ________________________ (tactic) was to ________________________ (secretly) plant an accomplice in the audience who would give "spontaneous" testimony to the healing powers of the medication for sale. The salesman and his partner usually left town immediately, before their audience could ________________________ (understand) that they had been tricked.

3 Writing or Discussion Activities

1. Several words in lessons 13 and 14 suggest underhandedness and deception. Use as many of the words listed below as you can to tell a story. Try not to retell the plot of a book or movie; invent your own story. Use any other words from the lessons that are useful to you.

> deflect
> rapacious
> surreptitious
> complicity
> duplicity
> apprehend
> reprehend
> reprisal

2. If you were to write a *reflection,* an informal account of something that you have been thinking about seriously, what subject would you choose? Montaigne* wrote about such subjects as fear, sadness, friends, anger, solitude, liars, smells, and clothing. He wrote about his own experience, his observations of others and the world, and his reading. Choose a subject about which you have something to say, using words from this lesson. The following words may stimulate your thinking:

> exploits (wonderful adventures?)
> ploys (tactics you or others have used to overcome an opponent?)
> apprehensions (worries? fears about the future?)
> dexterity (forms of dexterity you admire? kinds you possess?)

---

*French author Michel de Montaigne (1533–1592) wrote three books of essays.

LESSONS 15 AND 16

The Feet

LESSON 15

Manibus pedibusque.
With hands and feet (going into something "on all fours"; wholly; vigorously).

Familiar Words
biped
expedition
moped
pedal
pedestrian
pedicure
pioneer
quadruped

PES, PEDIS <L. "foot"

1. **expedient**   (ĕk spē′dē ənt)   [*ex* <L. "from," "out of"]

   adj. Appropriate to a purpose or useful in achieving a goal.

   Mary Ann Evans found it **expedient** to publish her novels under the name George Eliot.

   n. A means to an end.

   Limiting consumption of sugar and fatty foods is one **expedient** to physical fitness.

Challenge Words
expeditionary
millipede
pedicab
pied-à-terre
sesquipedalian

expediency, *n.*; **expediently,** *adv.*

2. **expedite** (ĕk′spə dīt′)   [*ex* <L. "from," "out of"]
tr. v. 1. To help or hurry the progress of something.

International cooperation can **expedite** a country's recovery after a serious earthquake or flood.

2. Of business, to perform business quickly.

Mobile phones allow busy executives to **expedite** transactions.

expeditious, *adj.*; **expeditiously,** *adv.*

3. **impede** (ĭm pēd′)   [*im = in* <L. "in"]
tr. v. To hinder; to block the way of.

Rival claims to territory have **impeded** a permanent peace in the Middle East.

impediment, *n.*

4. **pedigree** (pĕd′ə grē)   [*de* <L. "from," "away from," "down from" and *grus, gruis* <L. "crane": from the three-line, claw-shaped mark used to show succession in a pedigree]
n. 1. A line or list of ancestors, especially of a distinguished kind.

Burke's Peerage and Baronetage is a publication listing the **pedigree** of titled British citizens.

2. A recorded line of descent showing pure breeding of animals.

Living up to his distinguished **pedigree,** the bay colt Citation was the first horse to win the Triple Crown of American racing.

5. **pedometer** (pĭ dŏm′ə tər)   [*metron* <G. "measure"]
n. A device that calculates distance traveled by counting the number of steps taken.

The **pedometer** attached to the hiker's belt recorded a walk of ten miles.

POUS, PODOS <G. "foot"

6. **antipodes** (ăn tĭp′ ə dēs) [*anti* <G. "against"]
   n. 1. Any two places on opposite sides of the earth.

   China is the **antipodes** for most of the United States.

   2. Something that is the exact opposite of or contrary to something else.

   Charles Lamb observed that a beggar is always the **antipodes** to a king.

   antipodal, *adj.*; **antipode,** *n.*

7. **podiatry** (pə dī′ ə tre)
   n. The study and treatment of foot ailments.

   Podiatry includes the treatment of corns and bunions.

8. **podium** (pō′ dē əm) [*podion* <G. "small foot"]
   n. An elevated platform for an orchestra conductor or lecturer; a dais. (In biology, any foot-like structure.)

   In 1976 Sarah Caldwell became the first woman to mount the **podium** and conduct at the Metropolitan Opera House.

GRADIOR, GRADI, GRESSUM <L. "to step," "to walk"

9. **aggression** (ə grĕsh′ ən) [*ag* = *ad* <L. "to," "toward"]
   n. 1. The act or habit of launching attacks; invasion.

   Italy's **aggression** against Ethiopia began in 1936.

   2. Hostile action or behavior.

   Psychologists have set up **aggression**-prevention programs in many schools.

   aggressive, *adj.*; **aggressiveness,** *n.*

10. **degradation** (dĕg′ rə dā′shən) [*de* <L. "from," "away from"]
    n. 1. Reduction in rank or status, especially of office or dignity.

    During the Cultural Revolution in China from 1966 to 1976, many thousands of professional people suffered **degradation** at the hands of the Red Guard.

    2. Lowering of moral or intellectual character.

While Dorian Gray remains beautiful despite his moral **degradation,** his mysterious portrait grows increasingly hideous.

3. Disgrace; dishonor.

Because she failed to produce a male heir for Henry VIII, Catherine of Aragon suffered the **degradation** of divorce.

degrade, *v.*; **degraded,** *adj.*

11. **digress**   (dī grĕs´, dĭ grĕs´)   [*di = dis* <L. "away from," "apart"] *intr. v.* To stray from the main topic in writing or speaking; to turn aside.

Careful writers do not **digress** from the assigned topic on an exam.

digression, *n.*; **digressive,** *adj.*

12. **gradation**   (grā dā´shən) *n.* A systematic progression through a series of stages.

The **gradation** of colors in the spectrum moves from red to violet.

13. **gradient**   (grād´ē ənt) *n.* An incline or slope; the rate of incline.

The **gradient** of some streets in San Francisco is so steep that drivers must take special precautions when they park their cars.

14. **regress**   (rĭ grĕs´)   [*re* <L. "back," "again"] *intr. v.* To go back; to return to a former or less developed condition.

A new baby in the family sometimes causes older siblings to **regress** to babyish behaviors.

regress, *n.*; **regression,** *n.*; **regressive,** *adj.*

NOTA BENE: A word similar to *regress* is *retrogress;* its prefix *retro* <L. "backward" emphasizes the "return to an earlier condition," but suggests one that is worse, as in "After the fall of the Roman Empire, European civilization retrogressed."

EXERCISE 15A   Circle the letter of the best SYNONYM (the word or phrase most nearly the same as the word in bold-faced type).

1. the **gradient** of the road   a. rate of incline   b. surface
   c. condition   d. location   e. quality
2. the speaker on the **podium**   a. screen   b. platform   c. step
   d. ramp   e. stage

3. the greyhound's **pedigree**   a. health   b. footprint   c. owner
   d. breeding history   e. speed
4. the hiker's **pedometer**   a. device measuring distance walked
   b. device measuring foot size   c. device measuring walking speed
   d. device measuring foot pressure   e. shoe size

Circle the letter of the best ANTONYM (the word or phrase most nearly opposite the word in bold-faced type).

5. to **digress** in telling a story   a. grow tedious   b. stray   c. expand
   d. brag   e. keep to the point
6. controls that **impede** the driver   a. hinder   b. assist   c. imperil
   d. confuse   e. intrigue
7. continental **antipodes**   a. oversized feet   b. disagreements
   c. places at neighboring points on the globe   d. foot-race hurdles
   e. places at opposite points on the globe
8. to **regress** into adolescence   a. advance   b. decline   c. delve
   d. slip   e. relax
9. an act of **aggression**   a. domination   b. interference
   c. protection   d. resentment   e. invasion

EXERCISE 15B   Circle the letter of the sentence in which the word in bold-faced type is used incorrectly.

1. a. Victims of Alzheimer's disease steadily **regress** mentally and physically.
   b. After centuries of supremacy in engineering, law, and the arts, Roman culture began to **regress** when barbarians invaded Italy in 496.
   c. Some people live in the past; others prefer to **regress** into the future.
   d. Returning to her home town after thirty years, she was amazed by her **regression** to childhood sensations.
2. a. Arctic and Antarctic regions represent **antipodes** on our globe.
   b. Baseball and ballet seem **antipodal,** but performers in both must exert disciplined muscular control.
   c. He suffered from **antipodes:** one foot was larger than the other.
   d. Hard rock is the musical **antipodes** to chamber music.
3. a. Students can **expedite** the writing of term papers by finding a good subject quickly and taking notes efficiently.
   b. Several private companies compete with the U.S. Postal Service in **expediting** mail delivery.
   c. My cousin is an **expeditious** youngster who likes poking at wasps' nests and red ant colonies.

    d. Eleanor Roosevelt won praise as U.S. representative to the United Nations for her diplomatic and **expeditious** handling of difficult negotiations.

4. a. A frequent theme in the novels of French author Honoré de Balzac is the ultimate **degradation** of greedy young social climbers.

    b. Podiatrists recommend a **degradation** from high-heeled shoes to flats.

    c. Refugees fleeing a harsh government may suffer extreme hunger and **degradation** before finding a haven.

    d. The **degradation** of life on a battlefield defines the horror of war.

5. a. For many years, political, financial, and engineering uncertainties **impeded** the construction of a tunnel under the English Channel to connect England and France.

    b. Winston Churchill, one of the greatest orators of all time, suffered a speech **impediment.**

    c. The new car **impedes** faster than the old one.

    d. Amelia Bloomer's dislike of long skirts that **impeded** free movement led her in 1851 to introduce the "Bloomer costume"—a short skirt over pantaloons.

6. a. **Gradations** in radio frequency allow many stations to serve the same area.

    b. The Japanese beetle is a **gradation** of insect that damages fruit, flowers, and foliage.

    c. People with perfect pitch can detect the subtlest **gradations** of musical sounds.

    d. Rings in the trunks of trees record **gradations** in their growth.

EXERCISE 15C   Fill in each blank with the most appropriate word from Lesson 15. Use a word or any of its forms only once.

1. Stepping to the _____ , the candidate acknowledged the loud applause.

2. Because they weren't very interested in supply-side economics,

   students encouraged their teacher to _____ from the lesson.

3. When foot trouble becomes too painful, people turn to an expert in

   _____ .

4. Legal experts work to _____ the handling of court cases, which mount steadily in number

5. Although Germany and Russia had made a non-_____ pact, they became enemies in World War I.

6. Although the child seemed very mature, she _____ into temper tantrums when frustrated.

7. Breeders of exotic species of dogs keep a careful record of each

   animal's _____ .

8. When required to walk two miles a day, the survivor of open-heart

   surgery bought a(n) _____ .

LESSON 16

Aves omnes in pedes nascuntur.
All birds are born feet first.—PLINY

Key Words		
ambulatory	obstinate	restive
constituent	oust	stance
desist	preamble	static
destitute	recalcitrant	subsist
interstice	restitution	

Familiar Words
ambulance
somnambulist

Challenge Words
circumambulate
perambulate
perambulator

AMBULO, AMBULARE, AMBULAVI, AMBULATUM <L. "to walk around"

1. **ambulatory** (ăm′ byə lə tôr′ ē, ăm′ byə lə tōr′ē)
   adj. 1. Able to walk about.

   Although impeded by a cast, the patient was **ambulatory.**

   2. Pertaining to walking.

   Unattended skateboards are a hazard to **ambulatory** shoppers.

n. A place for walking; an arcade; a cloister.

Within Salisbury Cathedral there is a four-sided **ambulatory.**

ambulant, *adj.*; **ambulate,** *v.*

2. **preamble**   (prē′ăm bəl)   [*per* = *prae* <L. "before"]
   n. A preliminary statement in speech or writing; an introductory part.

The coordinator gave a brief **preamble** before the conference began.

CALCITRO, CALCITRARE, CALCITRAVI, CALCITRATUM
<L. "to kick"

3. **recalcitrant**   (rĭ kăl′ sə trənt)   [*re* <L. "back," "again"]
   adj. 1. Stubbornly resistant to authority or guidance.

Greek legend tells how Antigone's **recalcitrant** disobedience leads to her death.

2. Hard to manage.

An experienced trainer can teach the most **recalcitrant** animal to obey.

recalcitrance, *n.*; **recalcitrantly,** *adv.*

STO, STARE, STETI, STATUM <L. "to stand"
STATIO, STATIONIS <L. "a standing," "a standing position"
SISTO, SISTERE, STETI (also STITI), STATUM <L. "to cause to stand," "to put," "to place"

4. **constituent**   (kən stĭch′o͞o ənt)   [*con* = *cum* <L. "with"]
   adj. Serving as a necessary part of a whole.

The heart and lungs are **constituent** parts of the body.

n. A voter of a district represented by an elected official.

Members of Congress feel a responsibility to represent the wishes of their **constituents.**

5. **desist**   (dĭ zĭst′)   [*de* <L. "from," "away from"]
   intr. v. To cease doing something; to forbear; to abstain (often used with *from*).

Ignoring warnings that his health was threatened, César Chávez refused to **desist** from a hunger strike in support of farm workers.

6. **destitute**   (dĕs′tə to͞ot, dĕs′tə tyo͞ot)   [*de* <L. "from," "away from," "down from"]
   adj. 1. Altogether lacking.

Familiar Words
arrest
assist
circumstance
consistency
constant
constitute
Constitution
contrast
cost
distant
exist
insist
instant
obstacle
persist
resist
rest
stable
stage
stand
state
station
stationary
statistic
statue
status
substance
substitute
superstition

Challenge Words
extant
instate
obstetrics
reinstate
stanchion
statute

The refugees were **destitute** of hope.

2. Poverty-stricken.

Pearl Buck describes a **destitute** Chinese family in *The Good Earth*: Their fields bare and animals slaughtered, "indeed the man and his wife and his seven children had nothing to eat."

destitution, *n.*

7. **interstice**   (ĭn tûr′stĭs; plural **interstices**: ĭn tûr′stĭ sēz)   [*inter* <L. "between"]
n. Intervening space; a chink; a crevice.

The archaeologist discovered a fragment of ancient bone in the **interstice** between two rocks.

8. **obstinate**   (ŏb′stə nĭt)   [*ob* <L. "off," "against"]
adj. 1. Very stubborn; inflexible.

The stories of successful women in science have a common thread: their **obstinate** refusal to be turned away from their goals.

2. Difficult to control or subdue.

A conditioner helps control **obstinate** hair.

obstinacy, *n.*

9. **oust**   (oust)   [*ob* <L. "off," "against"]
tr. v. To force out of a position or place.

Voters **ousted** the corrupt judge.

ouster, *n.*

10. **restitution**   (rĕs tə tōō′shən, rĕs tə tyōō′ shən)   [*re* <L. "back," "again"]
n. 1. Restoration of a thing to its proper owner or its original state.

The crowning of Charles II in 1660 marked the **restitution** of the English monarchy after the interval of rule by the Commonwealth under Oliver Cromwell.

2. Repayment or repair for injury or damage.

The manufacturer made full **restitution** to consumers who had bought the faulty pedometers.

11. **restive**   (rĕs'tĭv)   [*re* <L. "back," "again"]
    adj. 1. Uneasy; restless.

    The class grew **restive** during the two-hour lecture.

    2. Unruly.

    Restive strikers clashed with the police.

    restiveness, *n.*

12. **stance**   (stăns)
    n. 1. The position of the body and the
    feet while standing.

    The guards at Buckingham Palace do not
    break their military **stance,** even when
    tourists ask them questions.

    2. An emotional or mental attitude.

    Actress Julie Harris's portrayal of Emily
    Dickinson captures the poet's **stance** of
    self-confident reticence.

13. **static**   (stăt'ĭk)
    adj. 1. At rest; unmoving.

    The drama critic charged that some scenes in the new play were
    static and therefore dull.

    2. Pertaining to electric charges.

    Clean hair may crackle with **static** electricity.

    n. Interference in radio and television signals as a result of electrical disturbances.

    Static frequently interrupted our favorite television program just at its
    climax.

    (Also slang: Disturbing or interfering remarks.)

14. **subsist**   (səb sĭst')   [*sub* <L. "under"]
    intr. v. 1. To exist; to be.

    Little plant life **subsists** above 20,000 feet.

    2. To be sustained; to live (used with *on* or *by*).

    Survivors **subsisted** for weeks on roots and berries.

    subsistence, *n.*

EXERCISE 16A   Circle the letter of the best SYNONYM (the word or phrase most nearly the same as the word in bold-faced type).

   1. **interstices** in the cell wall   a. growths   b. spaces   c. insects
       d. plasterings   e. messages
   2. **restive** horses   a. agile   b. hungry   c. eager   d. unruly
       e. obedient
   3. **recalcitrant** kindergartners   a. cooperative   b. unmanageable
       c. talkative   d. passive   e. unmotivated

Circle the letter of the best ANTONYM (the word or phrase most nearly opposite the word in bold-faced type).

   4. **ambulatory** sellers of goods   a. footsore   b. helpful   c. walking
       d. sluggish   e. stationary
   5. **obstinate** partners   a. irritable   b. inflexible   c. congenial
       d. flexible   e. clever
   6. **destitute** travelers   a. ambitious   b. impoverished   c. displaced
       d. reckless   e. well-to-do
   7. to **oust** an officer   a. force out   b. promote   c. install
       d. disregard   e. reassign
   8. a short **preamble**   a. early morning walk   b. warm-up exercise
       c. introduction   d. summary   e. conclusion
   9. a **constituent** element   a. remaining   b. nonessential   c. political
       d. vital   e. mechanical
  10. **static** conditions   a. unchanging   b. electrical   c. changing
       d. unusual   e. stable

EXERCISE 16B   Circle the letter of the sentence in which the word in bold-faced type is used incorrectly.

   1. a. Forbidden to marry, according to Roman legend, Pyramus and
           Thisbe talk through the **interstice** of a wall and secretly agree to
           meet at Ninus's tomb.
       b. Mountain climbers must be wary of **interstices** hidden by snow.
       c. A student looks to holidays as welcome **interstices** in the academic
           routine.
       d. Between acts in the ring, the clown **intersticed** the time by giving
           balloons to the children.
   2. a. Because the night was so balmy, she decided to **preamble** to the
           theater.
       b. At political conventions, delegates expect much **preamble** before
           the candidates appear on the podium.
       c. When buying a house, one must be sure to read the deed
           carefully, from **preamble** to closure.

      d. The first words of the **Preamble** to the United States Constitution are "We, the people of the United States."

3. a. In his poem "Bereft," Robert Frost refers to a "**restive** door" blown back and forth by the wind.

      b. The zoo keeper reported that many of the animals were **restive** just before the earthquake.

      c. An applicant for a job may grow **restive** and anxious while waiting to hear the outcome.

      d. Napping in her hammock, she spent a **restive** summer afternoon.

4. a. A wealthy patron helped the novelist James Joyce and his family to **subsist** until his works became well known.

      b. Because he is allergic to sunshine, he **subsists** under an umbrella.

      c. Before refrigeration was invented sailors **subsisted** for months chiefly on dried foods and hardtack, made of flour and water.

      d. Human history **subsists** in all of us, whether or not we are aware of it.

5. a. As soon as patients are **ambulatory,** the hospital releases them.

      b. When the weather was inclement, the monks strolled in the covered **ambulatory.**

      c. The sky divers were so severely injured that their companions called for an **ambulatory.**

      d. Living so far from public transportation, the villagers had to be **ambulatory** to get into town.

6. a. Although **destitute** of talent, the young actors made the rounds of every theater in New York.

      b. Her **destitution** was to make a name for herself on Wall Street.

      c. Vincent van Gogh was almost **destitute** at the end of his life; now his paintings sell for millions of dollars.

      d. English writer George Orwell explored lives of the **destitute** and downtrodden, recording his experiences in *Down and Out in Paris and London.*

7. a. The gastronome could not **desist** from eating all of the mouthwatering chocolate pie.

      b. The guards shouted at the brawlers to **desist** at once.

      c. Environmentalists urge companies to **desist** from manufacturing products that are not biodegradable.

      d. **Desist** me if you've heard this story before.

8. a. **Restitution** of damaged art works requires great patience.

      b. The U.S. government has offered **restitution** to American citizens of Japanese ancestry who were forced to live in internment camps during World War II.

      c. The injured jockeys stayed in a **restitution** until they were able to ride again.

      d. **Restitution** of earning power came slowly to many American writers blacklisted as Communists during the McCarthy era in the 1950s.

9. a. The soccer team improved its **stance** in the rankings at the end of the season.
   b. The ballerina's swanlike **stance** in *Swan Lake* brought ecstatic reviews.
   c. Throughout their trial the Salem women accused of witchcraft claimed they were wronged victims, a **stance** that modern historians consider justified.
   d. General MacArthur's rigid **stance** conveyed authority to soldiers under his command in World War II.

EXERCISE 16C   Fill in each blank with the most appropriate word from Lesson 16. Use a word or any of its forms only once.

1. In 1955 a group of army generals _____ Argentinian president Juan Perón in a military take-over.

2. During the siege of Leningrad, citizens _____ on scraps that were scarcely edible, even shoe leather.

3. Irate residents demanded _____ for the damage done by tree-trimmers to their exotic trees.

4. Members of Congress regularly send to their _____ a summary of issues that concern them.

5. The earth under us does not remain _____ ; the ground shifts continually.

REVIEW EXERCISES FOR LESSONS 15 AND 16

1 Circle the letter of the best answer to the following analogies and questions about roots and definitions.

1. *gradi* : to step : :
   a. *stare* : to stand
   b. *ambulare* : to climb
   c. *calcitrare* : to tap
   d. *sistere* : to walk
   e. foot : *pous*
2. preamble : before : :
   a. aggression : after
   b. subsistence : with
   c. regress : down
   d. destitute : away from
   e. interstice : under

3. aggression : hostility : :
   a. regression : advancement
   b. recalcitrance : obstinacy
   c. expedience : experience
   d. restitution : reprisal
   e. constituency : opposition
4. to expedite : to impede : :
   a. to impede : to degrade
   b. to digress : to wander
   c. to oust : to retain
   d. to desist : to stop
   e. to subsist : to hide
5. Which word does not derive from the Latin verb meaning "to step"?
   a. digress   b. gradient   c. graduate   d. regress   e. restive
6. Which word does not derive from the Latin word *pes, pedis?*
   a. expedient   b. impede   c. antipodes   d. pedigree   e. pedometer

2   Substitute the appropriate word from Lessons 15 or 16 for each word or phrase in parentheses in the following paragraphs. No word is used more than once.

1. The history of _____ (the treatment of the foot) records that serious foot and leg problems developed in the sixteenth century in Europe after the invention of shoes with heels. Although only one- to one-and-one-half inches high, they induced serious swelling of the calf, even requiring bandaging,

   _____ (interfered with) a person's pattern of

   _____ (walking), and caused a readjustment

   of his or her _____ (standing position). However, the variety of colors this new style of footwear came in— blue, red, green, saffron, and pink, as well as black and white—may have compensated for any discomfort.

2. During the nineteenth century, Great Britain used its colonies in

   Australia as a prison for its most _____

   (stubbornly resistant) criminals. Convicts were _____ (forced out) and were forbidden to return when their sentences were complete. While the country exported its criminals, it

   _____ (hurried the progress of) populating

   the new territory at the _____ (opposite side) of the globe.

3 Writing or Discussion Activities

1. The sentence that follows is long and awkward. Substitute seven of the words from Lessons 15 and 16 to make a concise sentence having no more than thirteen words, or even as few as eleven.

    Stubborn voters represented by an elected official manage to speed up the removal of an official for his slowing down the process of aid to poor farm workers who are without resources of any kind.

2. What sorts of occasions make you feel *restive? recalcitrant?* In a sentence or two for each word, describe situations in which those words apply to you. Be sure to include specific details.

3. What contrasts exist within your family, or within you yourself, that can be called *antipodes?* Write two or three sentences to illustrate the application of the word.

4. Write a sentence for each of the pairs of words below. Use the words in your sentences and give sufficient details to show a logical relationship between the words of each pair.
    a. restitution — aggression
    b. ambulatory — pedometer
    c. desist — obstinate
    d. regress — gradation

WORD LIST

(Numbers in parentheses refer to the lesson in which the word appears.)

ablution (7)
accolade (11)
accord (11)
acrophobia (5)
affront (9)
aggression (15)
allude (8)
ambidextrous (13)
ambulatory (16)
amicable (5)
amity (5)
anthropology (1)
antipathy (6)
antipodes (15)
apathy (6)
appease (5)
apprehend (14)
assiduous (12)
autocrat (1)
automaton (1)
autonomy (1)
autopsy (1)
avuncular (3)

bibliophile (5)
bigamy (3)

capitalist (9)
capitulation (9)
carnage (11)
carnivorous (8)
carrion (11)

cerebral (9)
cerebration (9)
collusion (8)
complacent (6)
complicity (14)
comprise (14)
concoct (8)
concordance (11)
confront (9)
congenital (2)
consanguinity (12)
constituent (16)
cordial (11)
corporal (11)
corporeal (11)
corps (11)
corpulent (11)
corpus (11)
covet (6)
cuisine (8)
cupidity (6)

decapitate (9)
décolletage (11)
deface (9)
deflect (13)
degradation (15)
deluge (7)
delusion (8)
dermatology (12)
desist (16)
destitute (16)

dexterity (13)
digital (13)
digress (15)
disgorge (10)
dissident (12)
divest (7)
domain (7)
domestic (7)
domicile (7)
domineer (7)
dominion (7)
dormant (7)
dorsal (12)
dossier (12)
duplicity (14)
dysentery (6)
dyslexia (6)

efface (9)
effrontery (9)
egoism (1)
elude (8)
emancipate (13)
empathy (6)
enamored (5)
endorse (12)
enervate (12)
engender (2)
entity (4)
entrepreneur (14)
epidermis (12)
essence (4)

euthanasia (4)
expedient (15)
expedite (15)
explicate (14)
explicit (14)
exploit (14)

facade (9)
facet (9)
familial (3)
feminism (1)
feminist (1)
fraternal (3)
fraternize (3)

gargantuan (10)
gargoyle (10)
gastric (12)
gastronome (12)
genealogy (2)
genesis (2)
genocide (2)
genre (2)
genteel (2)
gentile (2)
gentry (2)
genuflect (13)
gorge (10)
gradation (15)
gradient (15)
gynecology (1)

herbivorous (8)

heterogeneous (2)

homicide (1)

homogeneous (2)

humane (1)

humanism (1)

humanities (1)

hydrophobia (5)

imbibe (8)

impede (15)

implacable (6)

imply (14)

impregnable (14)

incarnate (11)

indentation (10)

indenture (10)

indigenous (2)

inexorable (10)

inflection (13)

ingenious (2)

inimical (5)

innate (4)

interstice (16)

investiture (7)

manacle (13)

mandate (13)

manifest (13)

manipulate (13)

matriarchy (3)

matriculate (3)

matrix (3)

mellifluous (8)

misanthrope (1)

misogamy (6)

misogyny (6)

monogamy (3)

moribund (4)

mortify (4)

naive (4)

nascent (4)

nonentity (4)

obstinate (16)

odious (5)

oracle (10)

oration (10)

orifice (10)

orthodontist (10)

orthopedics (4)

osculate (10)

ossify (11)

oust (16)

pacific (5)

pacify (5)

pathological (6)

pathos (6)

patriarch (3)

patrimony (3)

patronage (3)

patronize (3)

patronymic (3)

pedagogue (4)

pedant (4)

pedigree (15)

pedometer (15)

philanthropy (5)

phobia (5)

placate (6)

placid (6)

ploy (14)

ply (14)

podiatry (15)

podium (15)

postmortem (4)

potable (8)

potion (8)

preamble (16)

precipice (9)

precipitate (9)

precocious (8)

progenitor (2)

progeny (2)

puerile (4)

rapacious (13)

rapt (13)

recalcitrant (16)

recapitulation (9)

reflection (13)

regress (15)

regurgitate (10)

renaissance (4)

reprehend (14)

reprisal (14)

restitution (16)

restive (16)

saline (8)

sanguine (12)

seance (12)

sedentary (12)

somnambulate (7)

somnolent (7)

stance (16)

static (16)

subsist (16)

supercilious (10)

supersede (12)

supplicate (14)

surreptitious (13)

travesty (7)

trident (10)

uxorious (3)

vested (7)

vestment (7)

virile (1)

voracious (8)

xenophobia (5)